CATALOGUE
OF A
VALUABLE COLLECTION
OF
BOOKS ON AMERICA,
ILLUSTRATED WORKS, ETC.,

BELONGING TO

T. H. MORRELL,

CONSISTING OF

Rare Works on the History and Antiquities of America, early Printed Tracts, Franklin Imprints, and Washington Eulogies, together with a number of SUPERBLY ILLUSTRATED AND UNIQUE BOOKS, having inserted plates; Privately Printed and Large Paper Editions, etc.,

TO BE SOLD AT AUCTION,

On Tuesday, Wednesday and Thursday Evenings,
Jan. 12th, 13th and 14th, 1869,

By BANGS, MERWIN & CO.,

At their Salesroom 694 & 696 Broadway,

Commencing each Evening at 7 o'clock, precisely.

Gentlemen who cannot attend the Sale, may have their orders to purchase executed by the Auctioneers.

NEW YORK:
BERGEN & TRIPP, PRINTERS, 114 NASSAU ST.
1869.

NOTICE.

The Books forming this Collection have been selected with great care as to their condition, and comprise some of the choicest specimens of binding by Bedford, Riviere, Hayday, Matthews, Pawson and Nicholson, and other eminent Binders.

No Books have been admitted from my stock, or from any other source, and with the exception of a few volumes, none have ever been offered by me at private sale.

All are warranted perfect, unless otherwise described, and are offered without any reservation whatever.

The quotations of prices affixed to a large portion of the books, have been taken from priced Catalogues of the most prominent sales that have occurred in this city, and elsewhere, within the past ten years, and apply to copies similar in condition, unless otherwise stated.

The comparison of the fluctuations in the prices of many of the volumes, together with the uniformity of those realized by others, will it is hoped, be of interest to the Collector.

T. H. MORRELL,

100 NASSAU STREET.

New York, December 28th, 1868.

ERRATA.

Lot		
Lot	31	For *Price* read *Bruce.*
"	152	Omit *Frank.*
"	184	Omit *Morrell,* $3.25 ; *Bruce,* $2.75.
"	188	For *green* read *dark.*
"	206	For *Hewat* read *Hewatt.*
"	221	For $40 read $50.
"	243	Omit last *n* in *Presentationn.*
"	245	For 10 read 110.
"	311	For $5.00 read $3.00.
"	330	For *blue* read *green.*
"	533	For *very many* read *many very.*
"	565	Omit *by Matthews* after *laurels.*
		Insert *by Matthews* after *borders.*

A few errors occurring in punctuation, can readily be discerned.

Catalogue.

ADAMS, JOHN. Letters Addressed to his Wife. Edited by his Grandson, Charles Francis Adams. *Portrait.*—2 *vols.*, 12*mo*, *cloth*, *uncut.* Boston, 1841

2. ADAMS, MISS. Journal and Correspondence of, Daughter of John Adams, Second President of the United States. Written in France and England, in 1785. Edited by her Daughter. *Portrait, etc.* 2 *vols.*, 12*mo*, *cloth.* New York, 1841–2

3. ALDEN, Rev. TIMOTHY. Collection of American Epitaphs and Inscriptions, with occasional Notes. *Portraits.* 5 *vols.*, 12*mo*, *boards uncut, rough edges. Fine clean copy. Very Rare.* New York, 1814

Whitmore, $4.75 *per vol.;* Morrell, $4.75 *per vol.;* Roche, $4.12½ *per vol.*

4. ALEXANDER, GABRIEL. THE FAIR MAID OF WYOMING. A Tale of the War of Independence. Compositions from Campbell's Gertrude of Wyoming, by G. E. Hicks. With Introduction and Historical Notes. 13 *Beautiful Outline Engravings. Oblong,* 4*to.*, *cloth, gilt. Scarce.* Art Union of London, 1846

5. ALLEN, ETHAN. Narrative of the Capture of Ticonderoga, his Captivity and Treatment by the British. Written by Himself. *Fifth Edition, with Notes.* 8*vo.*, *uncut.* Burlington, 1854

6 ALLEN, IRA. Natural and Political History of the State of Vermont, one of the United States of America.

To which is added an Appendix containing answers to Sundry Queries, addressed to the Author. *8vo, pp.* 300, *boards, uncut, rough edges. Fine clean copy. Very scarce.* London, 1798

7 America Pois'd in the Balance of Justice. Ornamented with an *Elegiac* Frontispiece, and a *reconciliatory* Tailpiece. In this Research, the present Dissention between the Mother Country and her Colonies is considered in a new Light, and supported by Arguments quite different from those held forth by the parliamentary Speakers and polemical Writers on either Side of the Question. By P-oplicola H-istoricus. *Curious Emblematical Frontispiece and Tailpiece. 4to, pp.* 40, *half morocco.*
Rare. London, *Printed for the Author*, [1776.]

8 American Mariners; or the Atlantic Voyage, a Moral Poem. Prefixed is a Vindication of the American Character, from the Aspersions of the Quarterly Review. To which are added Naval Annals, etc. Copious Notes and Illustrations. *Thick post 8vo, uncut.*
London, n. d.

9 Anburey, Thomas. Travels through the Interior Parts of America. In a series of Letters. By an Officer. *Plates and maps. 2 vols. 8vo, boards uncut, rough edges. Fine copy, and very scarce in this condition.*
London, 1789

This copy contains the plates of the Continental Money, Vol. 2, p. 400, frequently wanting. "The Author was an Officer in Burgoyne's Army, and was taken prisoner by the Americans when that wing of the British Army fell into their hands. A graphic personal narrative."

Whitmore, $7. per vol.; Morrell, $5. per vol.

10 Andre, Major John. Cow-Chace, in Three Cantos, Published on Occasion of the Rebel General Wayne's attack of the Refugees' Block-House on Hudson's River,

on Friday, the 21st of July, 1780. *Rare and beautiful Portrait of Major Andre, inserted.* 8*vo, pp.* 69. *Full green crushed levant morocco, rich gilt back and sides, with inside borders, elaborately tooled, gilt top, uncut, by Matthews.*

New York, *Printed by James Rivington,* MDCCLXXX

The FIRST EDITION *of this celebrated Revolutionary lyric, a fine copy, perfect, and one of the rarest works ever offered for sale, It contains besides* "THE AMERICAN TIMES, *a Satire in Three Parts. In which are delineated the Characters of the Leaders of the American Rebellion, etc. By Camillo Quemo, Poet-Laureat to the Congress.*"

11 ANDRE. A representation of Major John Andre, Adjutant General to the King's Forces in North America, going from the Vulture Sloop of War to the Shore of Haverstraw Bay in the Hudson's River the night of the 23d of September, 1780, in a Boat which was sent for him (accompanied by a Mr. Smith,) under the Sanction of a Flag of Truce by Major General Arnold, who then commanded the Rebel Forces in that District. *Neatly mounted. Small folio, and bound in full crimson morocco.* "J. A. fec., 1st Oct., 1780."

EXCESSIVELY RARE.

The above is an exact copy of a drawing, sketched with a pen by Major Andre on the morning he was to have been executed, with a desire (it is supposed) of perpetuating a transaction which terminated fatally for him. The drawing was found upon his table, with other papers, the next day (being that of his decease,) by his servant, and delivered by him, on his arrival in New York, to Lieut. Colonel Crosbie, of the 22d Regiment, who caused this engraving to be taken, as a mark of his friendship for that unfortunate officer.

There is also inserted, a rare and beautiful Portrait of Major Andre, engraved by D. Berger, 1783.

12 ANDRE. ANDREANA. Containing the Trial, Execution and various matter connected with the History of MAJOR JOHN ANDRE, Adjutant General of the British Army in America, A. D., 1780. 12 *Fine plates, consisting of*

Portraits of Andre, Arnold, Paulding, etc., folio, uncut. Printed on heavy plate paper.

Philadelphia, 1865

LARGEST PAPER. 25 *Copies printed.*

13 ANDRE. DUNLAP, WILLIAM. ANDRE; a Tragedy in Five Acts, as performed by the Old American Company. New York, March 30, 1798. To which are added authentic documents respecting Major Andre; Letters to Miss Seward, etc. *Fine proof portrait of Dunlap inserted. 8vo. half morocco.* New York, 1798

Morrell, $20; Roche, $18.

14 ANDRE. Minutes of a Court of Inquiry upon the case of Major John Andre, with accompanying documents, published in 1780, by order of Congress. With an Additional Appendix. Edited by Franklin B. Hough. *Portrait, with 14 Plates inserted, including rare Portraits of Andre, Arnold, etc.; also original autograph signature of Major Andre. Small 4to, half morocco, gilt top, uncut.* Albany, 1865

100 *copies.* PRIVATELY PRINTED FOR MR. JOHN F. MCCOY.

15 ANDRE. SARGENT, WINTHROP. Life and Career of Major John Andre, Adjutant General of the British Army in North America. *Portrait. Thick 8vo; cloth, uncut.*

Boston, 1861

LARGE PAPER. 75 COPIES PRINTED.

Fisher, $15; Morrell, $12; Fowle, $11; Whitmore, $8.50; Roche, $8.

16 ANDRE. SMITH, JOSHUA HETT. An Authentic Narrative of the Causes which led to the Death of Major Andre, Adjutant-General of his Majesty's Forces in North America. To which is added a Monody on the Death of Major Andre, by Miss Seward. *Fine portrait of Andre, View of his Monument in Westminister Abbey*

and Map. 8vo, boards, uncut, rough edges. Fine clean copy: very rare. London, 1808

Morrell, $21; Fisher, $14.50, Roche, calf, $11.50.

17 ARCHENHOLTZ, J. M. VON. HISTORY OF THE PIRATES, FREEBOOTERS, OR BUCCANEERS OF AMERICA. Translated from the German. By George Mason, Esq. *Small 8vo, boards, uncut, rough edges.* London, 1807

18 ATLANTIC TELEGRAPH. Report of the Proceedings at a Banquet given to Mr. Cyrus W. Field, by the Chamber of Commerce of New York, at the Metropolitan Hotel, November 15th, 1863. *Portraits of C. W. Field, Peter Cooper, General Grant, and Admiral Farragut, and other Plates inserted. Also, Original Call for a Meeting of the American Geographical Society, "to coöperate with Dr. Hayes in organizing an Expedition to the Arctic Seas," signed by C. W. Field, Henry Grinnell, Peter Cooper, etc. 4to.* New York, 1866

LARGE PAPER.

19 AUSTIN, JAMES T. Life of Elbridge Gerry. With Contemporary Letters. To the close of the American Revolution. *Portrait and Fac-simile. 2 vols. 8vo, boards, uncut, rough edges.* Boston, 1828–'29

Fine, tall copy; very rare in uncut condition.

BAILY, J. T. Historical Sketch of the City of Brooklyn and the Surrounding Neighborhood, including the village of Williamsburgh and the towns of Bushwick, Flatbush, Flatlands, New Utrecht and Gravesend. To which is added an Interesting Account of the *Battle of Long Island.* Compiled from the best authorities. 12*mo.* Scarce.

Brooklyn: Published by the Author, 1840

21 Bailey, William. Records of Patriotism and Love of Country. *8vo, half green morocco; gilt back.* Washington, 1826

Scarce.

22 Bancroft, George. Poems. *Fine Portrait on India paper, and View of his residence at Northampton, Mass., inserted. 12mo, pp. 77; half morocco, gilt top, uncut.* Cambridge, 1823

Very scarce.

Davis, $41; Whitmore, $17.50.

23 Bancroft, George. Memorial Address on the Life and and Character of Abraham Lincoln, delivered at the request of both Houses of the Congress of America, before them in the House of Representatives at Washington, on the 12th of February, 1866. 15 *Portraits, all different, of President Lincoln, inserted; also beautiful proof portrait and fine autograph letter of Bancroft. 4to, half morocco, gilt top, uncut.* Washington, 1866

Large Paper.

24 Barber, John W. and E. G. Historical, Poetical and Pictorial American Scenes; with a Chronological Table of Important Events in the Secession War. *Map and numerous woodcuts. 12mo, uncut.* New Haven, n. d.

25 Barlow, Joel. The Columbiad: a Poem. *Beautiful Portrait of Barlow, and numerous Plates by Smirke, engraved by Heath, Bromley, etc. With three fine and rare Portraits and interesting Autograph Letter,* 2 *pp. 4to* (1811,) *of the Author inserted. Half green morocco, gilt top, uncut.* Philadelphia, 1807

Splendid copy, entirely free from stains, and of excessive rarity in uncut condition. Contains also the Fac-simile of the Signatures to the Declaration of Independence, often wanting.

26 Barnum, H. L. The Spy Unmasked; or, Memoirs of Enoch Crosby, *alias* Harvey Birch: being an Authentic Ac-

count of the Secret Services which he rendered his country during the Revolutionary War. (Taken from his own lips, in short hand), etc. *Portrait and Plates.* 8*vo*, *half green morocco*, *gilt top*, *uncut.*
New York, 1828

Wight, extra Plates, $14.50: Morrell, extra Plates, $11; Whitmore, $8.50; Fisher, $6.

27 Bartlett, John Russell. History of the Destruction of His Britannic Majesty's Schooner Gaspee in Narragansett Bay, on the 10th June, 1772. Accompanied by the Correspondence connected therewith. *Roy.* 8*vo.*, *uncut.* Providence, 1861

125 Copies privately printed.
Wight, $4.00.

28 Barton, William. Memoirs of the late David Rittenhouse, L.L.D., F. R. S., interspersed with various notices of many distinguished men. *Portrait.* 8*vo*, *boards*, *uncut.* Phil. 1813

29 Bartram, William. Travels through North and South. Carolina, Georgia, East and West Florida, the Cherokee Country, etc.; containing an Account of the Soil and Natural Productions of those regions; together with Observations on the Manners of the Indians. *Plates. Second Edition.* 8*vo*, *boards*, *uncut*, *rough edges.* London, 1794

Wight, $4.75; Fisher, half calf, $4.25; Morrell, $3.75.

30 Beacon Hill. A Local Poem, Historic and Descriptive, with Notes. *View of the Monument on Beacon Hill, Boston, inserted;* 4*to*, *pp.* 56, *uncut*, *rough edges. Very rare.* Boston, 1797.

Fine, clean copy.

31 Belknap, Jeremy. History of New Hampshire, comprehending the events of one complete century from the

discovery of the River Pascataqua. *Map.* 3 *vols.* 8*vo. boards, uncut, rough edges.* Dover, N. H., 1812

Slightly stained: volume 3 wants cover.
Price $4.50 per vol.; Whitmore, $2.50 per vol.

32 BENNETT, JAMES GORDON. Life and Writings of James Gordon Bennett, Editor of the New York *Herald. Woodcuts, with Portrait of Bennett inserted.* 12*mo. pp.* 64. New York, 1844

This scurrilous pamphlet is extremely rare, having been rigidly suppressed.

33 BENSON, EGBERT. DUTCH AND INDIAN NAMES. Memoir read before the Historical Society of the State of New York, December 31, 1816. *Illustrated by the insertion of* 15 *rare plates, including Portraits of Gen. Schuyler, Hendrick Hudson, etc., and Views of Nieuw Amsterdam, Hell Gate, Lake George, the Battery, Park Place, with curious old Map engraved by Tiebout, etc.* 8*vo, half green morocco, gilt top. Very rare.* New York, 1817

First Edition. Presentation Copy from Egbert Benson, with his autograph, and numerous manuscript corrections.

34 BENSON, EGBERT. DUTCH AND INDIAN NAMES. Memoir read before the Historical Society of the State of New York, December 31, 1816. Second Edition, with Notes. 12*mo, half morocco, gilt top, uncut, rough edges; rare.* Jamaica, 1825

Roche, $10; Morrell, $5.

35 [BEVERLY, RICHARD.] History of Virginia, in four parts. I. The History of the First Settlement of Virginia, and the Government thereof, to the year 1706. II. The natural Productions and Conveniences of the Country, suited to Trade and Improvement. III. The Native *Indians* and inhabitants, their Religion, Laws and Customs in War and Peace. IV. The Present State of the Country, &c. By a native of the place. *Second*

and best Edition. Arms of Virginia, and Plates by Gribelin, 8vo, calf. London, 1722

Fine clean copy, with large margins. Brilliant impressions of the Plates.

Bruce, $10.50; Whitmore, $10; Fisher, $10; Morrell, $5.

36 BIBLE. The Holy Bible, containing the Old and New Testaments, and the Apocrypha; Illustrated with Select, Rare and Curious Engravings after eminent Painters, and by the most celebrated Engravers, Ancient and Modern. *4 vols., folio. Full crimson levant morocco, rich gilt back and edges, with inside borders, by Hayday.* Glasgow, 1844

UNIQUE COPY, SUPERBLY ILLUSTRATED BY THE INSERTION OF OVER 500 EXTRA PLATES, *many of them being of the greatest rarity and beauty, and comprising some of the choicest specimens of engraving, by* VISSCHER, FAITHORNE, SAEDELER KILIAN, COLLAERT, GALL, KUSELL, A. WIERX, J. WIERX, *etc., etc.*

Many rare old etchings, curious colored plates, a beautiful set of illustrations from a French Bible, together with a number of the choicest of DORE'S *Plates, enrich these volumes, while the condition and brilliancy of the impressions of the Engravings could not be improved.*

An excessively rare etching (a folding plate), by JOHN LUYKEN, *of the "Shipwreck of St. Paul," and "Noah entering the Ark," by* VISSCHER, *may be mentioned as the most valuable.*

The text of this splendid work is BROWN'S IMPERIAL FAMILY BIBLE. *Extra Rubricated Title Pages have been printed especially for this work, which has been extended from* ONE *volume to* FOUR.

37 BIBLIOTHECA AMERICANA. Catalogue of a valuable Collection of Books, Pamphlets, Manuscripts, Maps, Engravings, etc., relating to America. Prepared by John Russell Smith. *8vo, half morocco, uncut.* London, 1865

38 BIRCH'S VIEWS. The City of Philadelphia, in the State of Pennsylvania, North America, as it appeared in the year 1800; consisting of twenty-eight plates. Drawn and Engraved by W. Birch & Son. *28 fine colored plates. Oblong folio, calf. Very rare. Published by subscription at $44.$\frac{50}{100}$.* Philadelphia, 1800

Slightly stained. Among the rare Engravings in this volume are views of Congress Hall, Pennsylvania Hospital, the Gaol, etc., with representation of the Funeral of Washington, Dec. 26, 1799.

39 Bishope, George. New England Judged, Not by *Man's*, but the *Spirit* of the Lord; and the summe sealed up of New-England's PERSECUTIONS. Being a *Brief* Relation of the *Sufferings* of the *People* called *Quakers* in *those* Parts of America, from the *beginning* of the *Fifth* Moneth, 1656, (the time of *their* first arrival at Boston from England), to the *later* end of the *Tenth* Moneth, 1660. Wherein the *Cruel Whippings* and *Scourgings*, *Bonds* and *Imprisonments*, *Beatings* and *Chainings*, *Starvings* and *Huntings*, *Fines* and *Confiscations* of *Estates*, *Burning* in the *Hand* and *Cutting* of *Ears*, *Orders* of *Sale* for *Bondmen* and *Bondwomen*, *Banishment* upon pain of *Death*, and *Putting* to *Death* of those *People*, are *shortly* touched with a *Relation* of the *Manner*, and *some* of the *other* most Material *Proceedings*; and a *Judgment* thereupon. *Small* 4*to*, *pp*. 176. *Original calf binding. Very scarce.*

London, 1661

Fine copy of the excessively rare first edition—a few pages very slightly stained, but otherwise in good condition.

40 Bishop, George. New England Judged by the Spirit of the Lord. In Two Parts. Containing a Brief Relation of the Sufferings of the People called Quakers, in New-England, from the Time of their first arrival there in the year 1656, to the year 1660. With a farther Relation of the Cruel and Bloody Sufferings of the People called Quakers in New-England, etc. Also an Appendix, Containing the Writings of Several of the Sufferers, etc., etc. *Thick* 8*vo*, *calf*, *gilt back*.

Fine Copy. *Very scarce.* London, 1703

Wight, $19.50; Morrell, $15; Bruce, $14; Fisher, $11.50.

41 Bleeker, Capt. Leonard. Order Book of Capt. Leonard Bleeker, Major of Brigade in the early part of the expedition against the Indian Settlements of Western New York, in the Campaign of 1779. Edited by Franklin B. Hough. *Portrait of Gen. James Clinton inserted. 4to, uncut.* New York, 1865

Large Paper. 50 *Copies printed.*

42 [Bloodgood, S. De Witt.] The Sexagenary; or Reminiscences of the American Revolution. *Rare and beautiful Portrait of Lady Ackland inserted.*
12*mo, boards.* Albany, 1833

Fine copy of the very rare original edition, of which but few copies were printed.

Morrell, $8.50; Roche, $5.

43. Border Life. Mirror of Olden Time Border Life; embracing a History of the Discovery of America, History of Virginia; also of the Early Settlement of Pennsylvania, with Personal Narratives of Captivities and Escapes, etc., compiled from authentic sources, by J. Pritts, Chambersburg, Pa. *Numerous plates of Indian Battles, Incidents of Border Life, etc.*
8*vo, sheep. Scarce.* Abbington, Va., 1849

Morrell, $4.

44 Boston Massacre. Short Narrative of the horrid Massacre in Boston; perpetrated in the Evening of the Fifth day of March, 1770, by Soldiers of the XXIXth Regiment, which, with the XIVth Regiment, were then quartered there. With some observations on the state of things prior to that Catastrophe. *Excessively rare Engraving of the Massacre, brilliant impression.* 8*vo, pp.* 166. *Full crimson levant morocco, gilt edges.* Printed by Order of the Town of Boston.
London, *Re-printed*, 1770

Fine copy, rare.

45 Boston Massacre. Hancock, John. An Oration delivered March 5, 1774, at the request of the Inhabitants of the town of Boston, to commemorate the Bloody Tragedy of the Fifth of March, 1770. *Original Lottery Ticket, for the Re-building of Faneuil Hall, Boston, April,* 1767, *signed by* John Hancock, *inserted; also an excessively rare and curious Portrait of him. Full rich green levant morocco, gilt.*
Boston: Printed by Edes & Gill, in Queen Street, 1774

Splendid copy, clean, with large margins. Once the property of Isaiah Thomas, *the Printer, and has his Autograph on title page.*

46 Boston Massacre. Orations delivered at the request of the Inhabitants of the Town of Boston, to commemorate the Evening of the Fifth of March, 1770, etc. 12*mo, sheep.* Boston, 1807

47 Boston Massacre. Short Narrative of the horrid Massacre in Boston; perpetrated in the evening of the fifth day of March, 1770, by soldiers of the 29th Regt., etc. *Plate of the Massacre.* 8*vo, cloth.*
Boston, 1770

New York: Re-published with Notes and Illustrations, by John Doggett, Jr., 1849.

Boston Massacre. [See Trial of Wemms.]

48 Boucher, Jonathan. View of the Causes and Consequences of the American Revolution, with an Historical Preface. *Thick* 8*vo, calf.*
London, 1797

49 Boylston, Zabdiel. An Historical Account of the Small-Pox, Inoculated in *New England,* upon all sorts of persons, *Whites, Blacks,* and of all ages and constitutions; with some account of the Nature of the Infection in the *Natural* and *Inoculated* way, and their dif-

ferent effects on *Human Bodies*, etc. *Small, 4to, pp. 62, Hf. calf. Fine copy, with large margins.* London, 1726

Among those mentioned as inoculated by the Author, may be found the names of Judge Quincy's Son, Judge Sewell's Grandson, Hon. Jonathan Belcher's Son, etc.

50 BOYNTON, EDWARD C. History of West Point and its Military Importance during the American Revolution; and the Origin and Progress of the United States Military Academy. *Illustrations and Maps, many on India paper. Roy. 8vo, cloth, uncut.* New York, 1864

LARGE PAPER. 100 *copies printed.*

Whitmore, $18; Fowle, $17.50; Morrell, $13.50; Fisher, $10; Roche, $8.

51 BRACKENRIDGE, H. M. History of the Western Insurrection in Western Pennsylvania, commonly called the Whiskey Insurrection, 1794. *8vo, cloth. Scarce.* Pittsburgh, 1859

52 BRADFORD, ALEXANDER W. American Antiquities and Researches into the Origin and History of the Red Race. *8vo, cloth.* New York, 1841

53 BREMER, FREDRIKA. Homes of the New World; Impressions of America. Translated by Mary Howitt. *3 vols., cr., 8vo, full polished green calf, gilt backs. Beautiful copy.* London, 1853

Fine plates.

54 BRUTÉ, SIMON WM. GABRIEL. Memories of the Right Reverend Simon Wm. Gabriel Bruté, D. D., First Bishop of Vincennes, with Sketches Describing his Recollections of Scenes connected with the French Revolution, and Extracts from his Journal. By the Right Rev. James

Rosevelt Bayley, D. D., Bishop of Newark. *Portrait and Illustrations. Small* 4*to, uncut.*
New York: John Gilmary Shea, 1860

Privately printed. 50 *copies.*
Roche, $5.00.

55 Bryan, Daniel. Mountain Muse; comprising the Adventures of Daniel Boone; and the Power of Virtuous and Refined Beauty. 12*mo, sheep.*
Harrisonburgh: Printed for the Author, 1813

56 Bucaniers of America, History of the. Containing the Exploits and Adventures of *Le Grand*, Lolonois, Roche Brasiliano, Bat the Portuguese, Sir Henry Morgan, etc. The *whole* written in several languages by persons present at the transactions. Translated into English. Fourth Edition. *Numerous Portraits and Plates.* 2 *vols. small* 8*vo, calf, gilt backs. Fine copy.*
London, 1741

57 Burgoyne, Lieut. Gen. State of the Expedition from Canada, as laid before the House of Commons by Lieut. General Burgoyne, and verified by Evidence; with a Collection of Authentic Documents, and an addition of many circumstances which were prevented from appearing before the House. Written and collected by himself, and Dedicated to the officers of the army he commanded. *Fine Map and Plans of Battles, with* 17 *rare and valuable Plates inserted, among which are Portraits of Burgoyne, Sir Guy Carleton, Gates, Baron Riedesel, etc., and also the very scarce folding plate of "Gen. Frazer's Funeral."* 4*to, half crimson levant morocco, gilt top, uncut.* London, 1780

Maps are all mounted on linen.

Fisher, *half morocco, uncut, no plates,* $19; Morrell, *half morocco, gilt edges, no plates,* $14.50.

58 Burgoyne, Lieut. Gen. [The Same.]

Fine Map and Plans of Battle, beautifully mounted on muslin. 8*vo*, *pp.* 191, *Appendix*, *pp.* CIX. *Boards, uncut, rough edges. Fine copy.* London, 1780

Gen. Charles Cotesworth Pinckney's copy, with his autograph on title page. Portrait of him inserted.

59 BURGOYNE, LIEUT. GEN. Letter from, to his Constituents, upon his late Resignation; with the Correspondences between the Secretaries of War and him relative to his return to America. 8*vo*, *pp.* 37, *boards, uncut, rough edges. Fine copy, rare.* London, 1779

After General Burgoyne's surrender, he was allowed to return to England on *parole.* Thinking himself ill-treated by the Government, and having been elected member of Parliament for Preston, he joined the opposition; whereupon an official order was sent to him, signifying that it was the king's pleasure that he should return to America and rejoin his captive army. He remonstrated, and was again ordered, and in consequence resigned all his civil and military employments. In this letter he gives an explanation of his conduct.

60 BURGOYNE. Orderly Book of Lieut. Gen. John Burgoyne, from his Entry into the State of New York until his Surrender at Saratoga, 16th Oct., 1777, etc. Edited by E. B. O'Callaghan, M. D. *Maps and Plates. Small* 4*to, uncut.*

MUNSELL'S HISTORICAL SERIES, NO. 7.

Albany, 1860

Fowle, half mor., uncut, $22; Whitmore, $9; Wight, $5.25.

BURGOYNE. Proceedings of a Courtmartial for the Trial of Col. Henley, accused by Gen. Burgoyne of Ill-Treatment of the British Soldiers.

SEE TRIALS.

61 BURK, JOHN. Bunker-Hill; or, The Death of General Warren. An Historic Tragedy, in five Acts. 12*mo, uncut.* New York, 1817

By the Author of the very rare "History of Virginia."

62 BURK, JOHN. History of the Late War in Ireland, with an

Account of the United Irish Association, from the First Meeting in Belfast to the Landing of the French at Kilala, *8vo, boards, uncut. Scarce.* Phila. 1799

Morrell, $3.00.

63 Burke, Edmund. An Account of the European Settlements in America, containing an Accurate Description of their Extent, Climate, Productions, etc., etc. New Edition. *Maps. 2 vols royal 8vo, boards, uncut, rough edges.* Large Paper. *Scarce.* London, 1808

Title pages slightly spotted.

64 Burr. Reports of the Trial of Colonel Aaron Burr (late Vice-President of the United States,) for Treason, and for a Misdemeanor, in preparing the means of a Military Expedition against Mexico, a Territory of the King of Spain, with whom the United States were at Peace, &c. By David Robertson. *2 vols. 8vo., boards, uncut, rough edges.* Fine Copy. *Very scarce.* Philadelphia, 1808

Bruce, $11.00 per vol.; Roche, $10.00 per vol.; Wight, half calf, uncut, $10 per vol.; Fisher, half mor., uncut, $9.00 per vol.; Morrell, half mor., uncut, $8.50 per vol.

65 Burr. Cheetham, James. Letter to a Friend on the Conduct of the Adherents to Mr. Burr. *8vo., pp. 72, half morocco.* New York, 1803

66 Burr. Cheetham, James. Narrative of the Suppression by Colonel Burr of the History of the Administration of John Adams, late President of the United States. Written by John Wood. To which is added a Biography of Thomas Jefferson, and of General Hamilton, with Strictures on the conduct of John Adams, and on the Character of General C. C. Pinckney. *8vo, pp. 72, half morocco.* New York, 1802

Wight, uncut, $5.00.

67 Burr. Cheetham, James. Nine Letters on the Subject of Colonel Burr's Political Defection, with an Appendix. *8vo, pp.* 130, *half morocco.* New York, 1803

68 Burr. Cheetham, James. Reply to Aristides. *8vo, pp.* 134, *half morocco.* New York, 1804

69 Burr. Cheetham, James. View of the Political Conduct of Aaron Burr, Esq., Vice President of the United States. By the author of the "Narrative." *8vo, pp.* 120, *half morocco.* New York, 1802

70 Burr. Examination of the Various Charges exhibited against Aaron Burr, Esq., Vice-President of the United States; and a Development of the Characters and Views of his Political Opponents. New edition, revised and corrected, with additions. By Aristides. *8vo, pp.* 116. *half morocco.*
Printed for the Author, 1804

71 Burr. Strictures upon the Narrative of the Suppression, by Col. Burr, of Wood's History of the Administration of John Adams. By a Yeoman. *8vo, pp.* 26, *half morocco. Very scarce.* s. l. s. a.

72 Burton. Bibliotheca Dramatica. Catalogue of the Theatrical and Miscellaneous Library of the late William E. Burton, the distinguished Comedian, comprising an immense assemblage of Books relating to the Stage; also, a small but select collection of Curiosities, Antiquities, Shakspearian Models, &c. *Fine Portrait. Thick Royal 8vo. uncut.*
Large Paper. New York. 1860

Morrell, half mor., uncut, $5.00; Fowle, $4.00; Whitmore, hf. mor., uncut, $3.50.

73 Butler, Frances Anne. Poems. *Beautifully engraved Portrait of Fanny Kemble, by Cheney, after Sully's Pic-*

ture. Portrait in the character of Euphrasia inserted; also Newspaper Cuttings. 12*mo, uncut.* Philadelphia, 1844.

Morrell, morocco, $5.00.

74 Butler, Mann. History of the Commonwealth of Kentucky, from its Exploration and Settlement by the Whites, to the Close of the Northwestern Campaign, in 1813. With an Introduction, etc. Second Edition; Revised and Enlarged by the Author. *Fine Portrait of Gen. George Rogers Clarke inserted. Thick* 8*vo., pp.* 551. *Half green morocco, gilt top, uncut. Fine copy. Scarce.* Cincinnati, 1836

Roche, cloth, uncut, $5.50; Fisher, sheep, $5.00.

75 Byfield, Nathaniel. An Account of the Late Revolution in New England. Together with the Declaration of the Gentlemen Merchants and Inhabitants of *Boston*, and the county adjacent, April 18, 1689. Written by Mr. Nathaniel Byfield, a Merchant of Bristol in New England, to his friends in London. *Small 4to, full crimson levant morocco, gilt back and edges, by Matthews.* London, 1689

Fine copy. Very scarce.

Morrell, $35; Roche, $30.

76 Byrd, William. Western Manuscripts; containing the History of the Dividing Line betwixt Virginia and North Carolina; a Journey to the Land of Eden, A. D., 1733; and a Progress to the Mines, written from 1728 to 1736, and now first published. *Roy.* 8*vo, uncut.* 1*st Edition scarce.* Petersburg, 1841

Fisher, Hf. Mor., uncut, $6.25.

CABOT, SEBASTIAN. Memoir of, with a Review of the History of Maritime Discovery. Illustrated by documents from the Rolls; now first published. 8*vo, boards uncut. Scarce.* London, 1831

78 CALLENDER, JOHN. An Historical Discourse on the Civil Religious Affairs of the Colony of Rhode Island and Providence Plantations, in New England, in America. From the first settlement, 1638, to the end of the First Century. 8*vo, full crimson levant morocco, gilt back and edges, with rich inside borders, by Bedford.* Boston, 1739

Beautiful copy of the very rare first edition.

Roche, $30 ; Morrell, $25.

79 CALLENDER, TOM. Letters to Alexander Hamilton, *King of the Feds ;* Ci-Devant Secretary of the Treasury of the United States of America, Inspector-General of the Standing Armies thereof, Counselor-at-Law, &c., &c., &c. Being intended as a reply to a *Scandalous Pamphlet,* lately published under the sanction, as it is presumed, of Mr. Hamilton, and signed with the signature of *Junius Philænus.* 8*vo, pp.* 64, *uncut. Fine, clean copy. Rare.* New York, 1802

Morrell, $5.50.

80 CAMPBELL, J. W. History of Virginia, from its Discovery till the year 1781 ; with Biographical Sketches of the most Distinguished Characters that occur in the Colo nial Revolutionary, or subsequent period of our History. 12*mo, calf.* Philadelphia, 1813

81 CAMPBELL, WILLIAM W. Annals of Tryon County ; or the Border Warfare of New York, during the Revolution. *Map.* 8*vo, boards, uncut, rough edges,* New York, 1831

Very rare, in uncut condition.

1 00 82 CAMPBELL, WILLIAM W. Border Warfare of New York, during the Revolution; or the Annals of Tryon County. 12*mo*, *cloth*. New York, 1849

2.00 83 CAREW, BAMPFYLDE-MOORE. Surprising Adventures of, King of the Beggars; containing his life, a Dictionary of the Cant Language, and many entertaining particulars of that extraordinary man. New edition, corrected and much improved. *Portrait and plates.* 12*mo*, *hf. cf.* London, 1812

3 00 84 [CARPENTER, STEPHEN CULLEN.] Memoirs of the Hon. Thomas Jefferson, Secretary of State, Vice-President, and President of the United States of America; containing a Concise History of those States, from the Acknowledgement of their Independence. With a View of the Rise and Progress of French Influence and French Principles in that Country. *Portrait and autograph letter of Jefferson* (Richmond, Nov. 26, 1780,) *inserted.* 2 *vols*, 8*vo*. *Hf. green morocco, gilt back.*

S. L. Printed for the Purchasers, 1809

A very scurrilous work, criticising severely the character and administration of THOMAS JEFFERSON.

Morrell, uncut, $5 *per vol.*; Wight, uncut, $3.75 *per vol.*

3 00 85 CARVER, JOHN. Travels through the Interior Parts of North America, in the years 1766, 1767, and 1768. *First edition. Maps and copper-plates. Royal* 8*vo*. *Boards, uncut, rough edges.*

Printed for the Author, London, 1778

LARGE PAPER. *Fine clean copy. Rare.*

Rare autograph receipt for enlisting five men, signed by Captain Carver, Springfield, May 31, 1760, *inserted; also portrait.*

Contains rare view of the Falls of St. Anthony, Mississippi River.

"Carver came to England soon after he returned from his travels, with the intention of publishing his account of them; but when he had already sold the MS. to a bookseller he was ordered by the government to deliver up all his maps and journals; and it was not until near ten years after that he obtained permission to publish the work."

86 CARVER, JOHN. Travels through the Interior Parts of North America, in the years 1766, 1767 and 1768. Third edition. To which is added some account of the author, and a copious index. *Beautiful Mezzotint Portrait, Map, and colored plates. Thick* 8vo, *bds., uncut, rough edges.* London, 1781

Fine copy.

86 CATESBY, MARK. Natural History of CAROLINA, FLORIDA, and the BAHAMA ISLANDS; containing the *Figures* of BIRDS, BEASTS, FISHES, SERPENTS, INSECTS, and PLANTS. Particularly the *Forest Trees, Shrubs,* and other *Plants,* not hitherto described, or very incorrectly figured by authors. Together with their descriptions in *English* and *French.* To which are added observations on the AIR, SOIL, and WATERS, etc., etc. Revised by Mr. EDWARDS, of the Royal College of Physicians, London; WITH THE SUPPLEMENT, *Map and* 200 *beautifully* COLOURED *plates of American Birds, Animals, Fishes, Insects, Plants, &c.* 2 *vols, Imperial folio, Russia gilt. Fine copy. Rare.* London, 1754

This edition is colored with superior care. Henry Laurens, of South Carolina, in 1780, says:—"the best Natural History of this country will be found in Catesby's book of Natural History, published by a Society of noblemen and gentlemen, about thirty-five years ago." See Laurens' Correspondence, page 187.

88 CATESBY, MARK. Hortus Britanno-Americanus; or a Curious Collection of *Trees* and *Shrubs,* the Produce of the British Colonies in *North America;* adapted to the *Soil* and *Climate* of England. With Observations on their Constitution, Growth and Culture, etc. 84 *beautifully colored Plates of Plants, etc., on* 17 *sheets. Imperial* 4to*; full morocco, gilt; specimen of old binding, with gilt tooling. Very scarce.* London, 1763

89 Caustic, Christopher. Terrible Tractoration! a Poetical Petition against Galvanising Trumpery, and the Perkinistic Institution. In Four Cantos. 12*mo, bds, uncut.* New York, 1804

90 Caustic, Christopher. Democracy Unveiled; or Tyranny Stripped of the Garb of Patriotism. 12*mo, boards, uncut.* Boston, 1805

91 Caustic, Christopher. [The same.]
Third Edition, with large additions. 2 *vols.* 12*mo, hf. crimson morocco, gilt top, uncut.* New York, 1806

92 Chalkley, Thomas. Collection of the Works of, In Two Parts. 2 *vols.* 8*vo. Full crimson levant morocco, richly tooled back, and inside borders, by Bedford. Very rare.*
Philadelphia: Printed by B. Franklin & D. Hall, MDCCXLIX.

Wight, $10 per vol.

93 Chalmers, George. Political Annals of the Present United Colonies, from their Settlement to the Peace of 1763. Compiled chiefly from Records, and Authorized often by the insertion of State Papers. *Autograph Letter of the Author inserted. Vol.* 1, *all published. Thick* 4*to, full brown levant morocco, gilt edges.* David Ramsay's *(the historian) copy, with his autograph on title page. Portrait of him inserted.* London, 1780

"Valuable for the distinctness of its details, the authenticity of its documents, and the elegant manner in which it is written."

Fisher, half mor., uncut, Portrait inserted, $19; Wight, half mor., uncut, $12.50.

94 Charlevoix. History and General Description of New France. By the Rev. P. F. X. De Charlevoix, S. J.

Translated, with Notes, by John Gilmary Shea. *Portraits and Maps.* 3 *vols.* 4*to, uncut.*

New York, 1866–1868

LARGE PAPER. Only 25 copies printed.

The purchaser to be entitled to the remaining volumes (3) at the subscription price.

Morrell, $9.50 per vol.

95 CHARLEVOIX. [The Same.]

Portrait and Maps. 3 *vols. Imperial* 8*vo, uncut.*

New York, 1866–1868

250 COPIES PRINTED..

The purchaser to be entitled to the remaining volumes (3) at the subscription price.

Morrell, $5.00 per vol.

96 CHASTELLUX, MARQUIS DE. Travels in North America, in the years 1780, 1781 and 1782. Translated from the French by an English Gentleman who resided in America at that period. With notes by the Translator. *Maps and Plates, with Portrait of the Author inserted.* 2 *vols,* 8*vo, Hf. calf, gilt backs, uncut.*

London, 1787

Fine copy, and scarce in this condition.

Morrell, $3 *per vol.*

97 CHESS MADE EASY. New and Comprehensive Rules for Playing the Game of Chess; with Examples from Philidor, Cunningham, etc., etc. To which is prefixed a pleasing account of its origin; some interesting anecdotes of several exalted personages, who have been admirers of it, and the *Morals of Chess.* Written by the ingenious and learned Dr. FRANKLIN. *Plate. Rare Portrait of Dr. Franklin inserted.* 12*mo, full purple crushed levant morocco, gilt edges, by Pratt.*

Philadelphia, 1802

Scarce.

98 Cicero, M. T. Cato Major, or his Discourse of Old Age; with Explanatory Notes. (By John Logan.) *8vo, full green crushed levant morocco, richly gilt back and inside borders, by Bedford.* Philadelphia, *printed and sold by B. Franklin.* MDCCXLIV

This book Franklin always considered the *chef d'œuvre* of his press. "He took many copies to England, and distributed them with evident satisfaction."

Beautiful copy. Very scarce.

Bruce, $90; Wight, *MSS. of Franklin inserted,* $73.

99 Clinton, Sir Henry and Cornwallis, Earl. Narrative of Lieutenant-General Sir Henry Clinton, K. B., Relative to his Conduct during Part of his Command of the King's Troops in North America, etc. *Rare and beautiful Portrait of Sir Henry Clinton inserted.*

Answer to that part of the Narrative of Lieutenant-General Sir Henry Clinton, K. B., which relates to the conduct of Lieutenant-General Earl Cornwallis, during the Campaign in North America, in the Year 1781. *Fine Portrait of Cornwallis inserted.*

Observations on some parts of the answer of Earl Cornwallis to Sir Henry Clinton's Narrative, etc. *Fine Portrait of Sir Henry Clinton inserted.* 3 *vols,* 8*vo, half green crushed levant morocco, gilt top, uncut.* London, 1783

Clean, uncut copies of these rare pamphlets.

Morrell, *bound together in one volume,* $20; Roche, the same, $19.50.

100 Clinton, Sir Henry and Cornwallis, Earl. Narrative of Lieutenant-General Sir Henry Clinton, K. B., Relative to his Conduct during part of his Command of the King's Troops in North America, etc.

Answer to that part of the Narrative of Lieutenant-General Sir Henry Clinton, K. B., which relates to the Conduct of Lieutenant-General Earl Cornwallis during the Campaign in North America, in the Year 1781.

Observations on some parts of the answer of Earl Cornwallis to Sir Henry Clinton's Narrative, etc. 3 *vols*, 4*to*, *uncut*. Large Paper. 75 *copies printed.* Philadelphia, 1865–66

The above were re-printed from the London Editions, 1783.

101 Cloquet. M. Jules. Recollections of the Private Life of General Lafayette. *Numerous wood-cuts.* 5 *rare and beautiful Portraits of Lafayette inserted.* 8*vo cloth*, *uncut.* London, 1835

102 [Cockings, George.] The American War; a Poem. In Six Books. In which the names of the officers who have distinguished themselves during the war are introduced. *Extremely rare Print of the "Attack on Bunker's Hill, etc."* 8*vo*, *half calf.* London, 1781

Roche, half morocco, uncut, $8.50.

103 Coghlan, Mrs. Memoirs of, (daughter of the late Major Moncrieffe). Written by herself, and dedicated to the British Nation; being interspersed with Anecdotes of the late American and present French War. With Remarks, Moral and Political. *Portrait of Aaron Burr inserted.* 2 *vols. in one.* *Small* 8*vo*, *half Russia. Scarce.* London, 1794

Large type. Fine, clean copy.

104 Coghlan, Mrs. [The same.] *small* 8*vo*, *calf.* London, 1794

105 Coghlan, Mrs. Memoirs of, (daughter of the late Major Moncrieffe). Written by herself, and dedicated to the British Nation; being interspersed with Anecdotes of the late American and present French War. With Remarks, Moral and Political. *Small* 8*vo*, *full smooth calf, gilt back and edges, by Pratt. Rare.*

New York: T. & J. Swords, 1795

Contains the New York Preface, suppressed, and nearly always wanting.

Morrell, extra plates, $28,00; Wight, $6.25.

Roche, " " 28.50.

106 Coghlan, Mrs. [The same.] 22 *Plates inserted. including rare Portraits of Gens. Amherst, Monckton, Montgomery, Cornwallis, Geo. III., etc.; some proofs on India paper. Also very scarce Autograph Letter of Major Moncrieffe, Father of Mrs. Coghlan.* 1 *page* 4*to.* Charlestown, 1780. 8*vo, full crimson morocco, gilt top, uncut.*
100 *copies reprinted, with Introduction and Notes.*
New York: T. H. Morrell, 1864

107 Colden, Cadwallader. The History of the *Five Indian Nations of Canada*, which are the barrier between the English and French in that part of the World, etc. Second Edition. *Map.* 8*vo, half Russia.*
Fine copy. London, 1750
Wight, $7; Morrell, $4,

108 Colden, Cadwallader. The History of the Five Indian Nations of Canada, which are dependent on the Province of New York, in America, etc. Third Edition. *Map.* 2 *vols.*, 12*mo, calf.* London, 1755
Morrell, $3.00 per vol.; Fisher, $2.62 per vol.

109 Colden Cadwallader. The History of the Five Indian Nations Depending on the Province of New York. *Reprinted exactly from* Bradford's New York Edition, 1727. With an Introduction and Notes by John Gilmary Shea. *Portrait.* 8*vo, full rich brown morocco, bevelled, gilt top, uncut.*
125 *copies printed.* New York: T. H. Morrell, 1866
Portrait of Gov. Burnet, and Map of the "Five Great Lakes" inserted.

110 Colden, Cadwallader. The History of the Five Indian Nations Depending on the Province of New York. *Reprinted exactly from* Bradford's New York Edition (1727). With an Introduction and Notes by John

Gilmary Shea. *Portrait on India paper. Imperial 8vo, cloth, uncut.*

LARGE PAPER; *only* 30 *Copies printed.*

New York: T. H. Morrell, 1866

Morrell, $16; Roche, $9.

111 COLDEN, CADWALLADER D. Memoir, prepared at the request of a Committee of the Common Council of the City of New York, and Presented to the Mayor of the City at the Celebration of the Completion of the New York Canals. *Fine Portraits of Colden, Philip Home, S. L. Mitchell, etc., engraved by Durand. Maps, Plans, Views, etc., etc.* 4*to, boards, uncut, rough edges.*

New York, 1825

Fine, clean copy, very rare, in uncut condition. It may not be well known that the narrative was written by the late Mr. Wm. L. Stone, of whom a very rare portrait is inserted in this copy.

Morrell, $14.50.

112 COLUMBIAN MUSE. A Selection of American Poetry, from various Authors of Established Reputation. *Portrait of Joel Barlow, fine old impression, inserted.* 12*mo, sheep.* New York, 1794

Fine copy of this scarce little volume.

Morrell, morocco, $10; Fisher, $4.25.

113 CONDUCTOR GENERALIS; or, the Office, Duty and Authority of Justices of the Peace, High-Sheriffs, Under-Sheriffs, Gaolers, Coroners, Constables, Jurymen, and Overseers of the Poor. As also the Office of Clerks of Assize and of the Peace, etc. To which is added a Collection out of *Sir Matthew Hales*, etc. Second Edition, with large Additions. 8*vo, pp.* 592, *half calf, antique, red edges.*

Philadelphia: Printed and sold by B. FRANKLIN and D. HALL, at the New *Printing Office*, near the Market, 1749

Wight, $10.

114 CONSTITUTIONS (THE) OF THE SEVERAL INDEPENDENT STATES OF AMERICA; the Declaration of Independence; the Articles of Confederation between the said States; the Treaties between His Most Christian Majesty and the United States of America. Published by order of Congress. 12*mo*, *pp.* 226, *original sheep binding.*

ONLY 200 COPIES PRINTED. *Very rare.*

Philadelphia, 1781

The following notice, from page 2, will show that this is a work of the deepest historical and political interest, as the *first authoritative* and *original printed text* of these important documents.

"In Congress, December 29, 1780. Resolved, That a Committee of three be appointed to collect and cause to be published *two hundred correct copies* of the Declaration of Independence, etc. (as in title above), to be bound together in boards, etc., etc.

" Extract from the Minutes. CHARLES THOMPSON, Secretary."

Morrell, *uncut copy*, $20 ; Welford, $13.

115 CONSTITUTIONS OF THE SEVERAL INDEPENDENT STATES OF AMERICA; the Declaration of Independence, and the Articles of Confederation between the said States, etc. The whole arranged, with a *Preface* and *Dedication* by the Rev. William Jackson. Second Edition. *Rare and Curious Portrait of Washington, with emblematical design, Flags, Liberty Cap and Serpent, and Motto, " Don't tread on me," engraved by Sharp.* 8*vo*, *pp.* 472, *boards, uncut, rough edges.*

Scarce, London, Stockdale, 1783

116 COOPER, J. FENIMORE. History of the Navy of the United States of America. 50 *Portraits, Views, etc., collected for insertion; also Autograph Note of Cooper, and Letters signed by Commodores Stewart and Warrington.* 2 *vols.* 8*vo*, *cloth, uncut. Fine, large type edition.*

London, 1839

117 COOPER, Rev. Mr. History of North America; containing a Review of the Customs and Manners of the Original

Inhabitants, the First Settlement of the British Colonies, etc. *Curious Copper Plates of the Death of Gen. Montgomery, Defeat of De Grasse, Destruction of Tea at Boston, etc.* 12*mo*, *pp*. 184, *unbound*.
Scarce. London, 1789

118 COXE, DANIEL. Description of the English Province of Carolana, by the Spaniards called Florida, and by the French La Louisiane. As also of the great and famous river Meschacebe, or Mississippi, the five vast navigable Lakes of Fresh Water, and the Parts Adjacent, etc., and a Preface. *Fine Map.* 8*vo*, *boards*.
London, 1722
Reprinted, St. Louis, 1840

119 CURTIS, G. W. LOTUS EATING. A Summer Book. *Beautiful Woodcuts from Designs by J. F. Kensett. Portrait inserted.* 12*mo*, *uncut*. *Scarce.*
New York, 1852

DARTMOOR PRISON. ANDREWS, CHARLES. The Prisoners' Memoirs; or, Dartmoor Prison: Containing a complete and impartial History of the entire Captivity of the Americans in England, etc. Also, a Particular Detail of all Occurrences Relative to that Horrible Massacre at Dartmoor, on the fatal evening of the 6th of April, 1815. *Colored View of Dartmoor Prison.* 12*mo*, *half calf, gilt top, uncut, rough edges.*
New York: Printed for the Author, 1815

Morrell, $4.25; Fisher, $4.00.

121 DARTMOOR PRISON. Journal of a Young Man of Massachusetts, late a Surgeon on board an American Privateer who was captured at sea by the British, in May,

1813, and was confined, first, at Melville Island, Halifax, then at Chatham, in England, and last, at *Dartmoor Prison;* interspersed with Observations, Anecdotes and Remarks. Written by himself. *Folding Plate of Dartmoor Prison, representing the Massacre of American Prisoners.* 12*mo, sheep. Scarce.*
Boston, 1816

Fisher, $2.75.

122 Dartmoor Prison. The Prisoners' Memoirs; or Dartmoor Prison: Containing a Complete and Impartial History of the Entire Captivity of the Americans in England, etc., with a Particular Detail of the Horrid Massacre at Dartmoor on the Fatal Evening of the 6th of April, 1815. The whole carefully compiled by a Prisoner in England, who was a Captive during the whole war. 12*mo, cloth.*
New York: Printed for the Author, 1852

Morrell, $3.50.

123 Davies, Samuel. Religion and Patriotism the Constituents of a Good Soldier. A Sermon Preached to Captain Overton's Independent Company of Volunteers raised in Hanover County, Virginia, August 17, 1755. By Samuel Davies, A. M., Minister of the Gospel there. 8*vo, half morocco, gilt edges.* London, 1756

This rare Sermon contains the following prophetic note on page 12. "*As a remarkable instance of this, I may point out to the public that heroic youth,* Col. Washington, *whom I cannot but hope Providence has hitherto preserved in so signal a manner for some important service to his country.*"

Morrell, $5.50.

124 Davis, W. H. H. History of the Battle of the Crooked Billet, fought May 1st, 1778. 8*vo.*
Scarce. Doyleston, Pa., 1860

125 Davis. Catalogue of the Entire Private Library of the late Mr. William J. Davis, with "In Memoriam;" being a

Biographical Sketch of William Jackson Davis, by Henry B. Dawson, Esq. *Portrait.* 2 *vols.* 4*to*, *uncut.* New York, 1865

LARGE PAPER ; 75 *copies printed.*
Morrell, $2.00 per vol.

126 DAWSON, HENRY B., GRISWOLD, A. CLIFFORD, and others. Major-General Israel Putnam. A Correspondence on this subject with the Editor of the *Hartford Daily Post*, by "Selah," of that city, and Henry B. Dawson, of White Plains, N. Y. ILLUSTRATED COPY, *having* 47 *Plates inserted, including eight different Portraits of Gen. Putnam, some being of extreme rarity ; also Portraits of Gens. Reed, Wooster, Green, Stark, Dearborn, Major Rogers, Drs. Styles, Belknap, Dwight and others ; and a number of Curious Views of the Battle of Bunker Hill, Putnam's Escape at Horseneck, etc. Many of the Engravings are Proofs on India Paper. Full green levant morocco, rich gilt back and sides, with inside borders, gilt top, uncut.*
LIMITED EDITION. Morrisania, N. Y., 1860

Very Scarce. 117 *copies of the* 252 *only printed, having been destroyed by fire.*
Morrell, half morocco, extra plates, $32.50.

127 DAWSON, HENRY B., GRISWOLD, A. CLIFFORD, AND OTHERS. Major-General Israel Putnam. A Correspondence on this Subject with the Editor of *The Hartford Daily Post*, by "Selah," of that City, and Henry B. Dawson, of White Plains, N. Y. *Royal* 8*vo*, *uncut.*
LIMITED EDITION. Morrisania, N. Y., 1860.

Fowle, $30. Wight, half Russia, $14.

128 DAWSON, HENRY B. The Assault on Stony Point by General Anthony Wayne, July 16, 1779. Prepared for the New York Historical Society, and read at its regular

monthly meeting, April 1, 1862. *With a Map, Fac-similes, and Illustrative Notes. Royal* 8*vo, uncut.* Morrisania, N. Y., 1863

LIMITED EDITION; *only* 250 *Copies printed.*
Fowle, $20.50; Morrell, half morocco, extra plates, $20.

129. DAWSON, HENRY B. Battles of the United States by Sea and Land. *Fine Steel Plates.* 40 *numbers, uncut,* 4*to, as originally published.* New York, 1858

SUBSCRIBERS' COPY.

130 DAWSON, HENRY B. Sons of Liberty in New York: A Paper read before the New York Historical Society, May 3d, 1859. *Portrait of Cadwalader Colden inserted.* 8*vo, uncut.* New York, 1859

PRIVATELY PRINTED; *limited edition.*
Morrell, half morocco, $4.

131 DE GRASSE. The Operations of the French Fleet, under the Count De Grasse in 1781-2, as described in two contemporaneous journals. *Portrait on India paper, etc, with* 10 *plates inserted, including fine Portraits of De Grasse, D'Estaing, Rochambeau, and others, and three very rare Prints representing the "Defeat of De Grasse by Lord Rodney, in* 1782." *Royal* 8*vo, cloth, uncut.* New York, 1864

PRIVATELY PRINTED; 150 *copies Bradford Club Series No.* 3.
Morrell, extra plates, $25.

132 DELEPLAINE. Repository of the Lives and Portraits of Distinguished American Characters. 18 *Portraits; Washington, Hamilton, Jay, Henry Laurens, Peyton Randolph, etc.* 3 *vols,* 4*to, boards, uncut, rough edges.* Philadelphia, 1815-18

Fine copy in the parts, as originally published. Beautiful impressions of the plates,
Morrell, Autograph Letter inserted, $7 per vol.

133 DENTON, DANIEL. Brief Description of New York, formerly called New Netherlands, with the Places Thereunto Adjoining. Likewise a Brief Relation of the Customs of the Indians there. *New Edition, with an Introduction, and copious Historical Notes, by Gabriel Furman. 4to, cloth, uncut.*

New York, 1845

LARGE PAPER; 100 *copies printed.*
Morrell, $3.50.

134 DE SOLIS, DON ANTONIO. The History of the Conquest of Mexico by the Spaniards. Done into English from the Original Spanish, by Thomas Townsend, Esq. *Plates, with fine Portrait of Cortez, engraved by Vertue, after Titian. Folio, Panelled calf; fine copy.*

London, 1724

Morrell, $4.50.

135 DE SOTO. Narratives of the Career of Hernando De Soto in the Conquest of Florida, as told by a Knight of Elvas, and in a Relation by Luys Hernandez de Biedma, Factor of the Expedition. Translated by Buckingham Smith. *Portrait on India paper, map, etc. Engraving of the Burial of De Soto inserted. Imperial 8vo, uncut.*

New York, 1866

75 COPIES ONLY PRINTED.
Bradford Club Series, No. 5. Has view of William Bradford's Tombstone in Trinity Church-yard.
Morrell, $14.

136 DETAIL OF SOME PARTICULAR SERVICES PERFORMED IN AMERICA, During the Years 1776, 1777, 1778 and, 1779. Compiled from Journals and Original Papers, supposed to be chiefly taken from the Journal kept on Board of the Ship Rainbow, Commanded by Sir George Collier, while on the American Station during that Period. *12mo, cloth, uncut.*

New York, 1835

PRIVATELY PRINTED FOR ITHIEL TOWN.
Fine, clean copy of this very scarce little book.
Morrell, $4.

137 Dickinson, John. Political Writings. *Portrait, View of Dickinson College, and rare Document, signed,* 1760, *inserted.* 2 *vols.,* 8*vo, sheep.*
Wilmington, 1801

138 Doddridge, Rev. Dr. Joseph. Notes on the Settlement and *Indian Wars* of the Western Parts of *Virginia* and *Pennsylvania,* from the Year 1763 until the Year 1783 inclusive. Together with a View of the State of Society and Manners of the First Settlers of the Western Country. 12*mo, sheep, fine copy, scarce.*
Wellsburg, Va., 1824

Fisher, $6.62; Morrell, $6.

139 Dorr, Rev. Benjamin. Memoir of John Fanning Watson, the Annalist of Philadelphia and New York. Prepared by Request of the Historical Society of Pennsylvania, and read in their Hall, Monday Evening, February 11, 1861. *Portrait (photograph).* 8*vo, cloth.*
Philadelphia, 1861

But few copies printed.

140 Drake, Joseph Rodman, and Halleck, Fitz-Greene. The Croakers. First complete edition. *Portraits on India paper. Portrait, engraved by Burt from Roger's beautiful Miniature (Private Plate), and Autograph Letter of Halleck inserted, also Dr. Shelton Mackenzie's Review of the Work, from the Philadelphia Press, Nov.* 9, 1860, *and other cuttings. Royal* 8vo., *full maroon morocco, gilt top, uncut.*
New York, 1860

Privately Printed; 150 copies.
Bradford Club Series, No. 2.
Morrell, cloth, $12.50.

141 Drake, Samuel G. Book of the Indians; or, Biography and History of the Indians of North America, from its First Discovery to the Year 1841. Eighth edition,

with large additions and corrections. *Portraits, Maps, etc. Thick* 8*vo, cloth, uncut.*
Boston, 1841

Contains the Portraits of Sir William Johnson, Gen. Wayne, Red Jacket, Pocahontas, etc., omitted in subsequent editions.

Morrell, $6.50 ; Roche, $5.

142 DRAKE, SAMUEL G. A Brief Memoir of Sir Walter Raleigh, prepared for and published in the N. E. Historical and Genealogical Register for April, 1862, and now reprinted with additions. *Portrait after Zucchero. Royal* 4*to, full crimson levant morocco, richly gilt sides and inside borders, by Pawson and Nicholson.*
Boston : Printed for the Author for Private Distribution.
1862

LARGE PAPER ; *only* 10 *copies printed.*

One of the finest specimens of Pawson and Nicholson's binding. Rare Portrait of Raleigh, engraved by Simon Pass, original impression, inserted.

Morrell, extra plates, $23 ; Fowle, $19.

143 DRAKE, SAMUEL G. The History and Antiquities of Boston, the Capital of Massachusetts, and Metropolis of New England, from its Settlement in 1630 to the year 1770. Also an Introductory History of the Discovery and Settlement of New England. With Notes Critical and Illustrative. 42 *fine steel Plates, Portraits, Views, etc., with several hundred Woodcuts.* 2 *vols., folio sheets, folded.*
Boston, 1857

LARGE PAPER ; *but few printed, scarce.*

Has also the Portrait of Samuel G. Drake, the author, taken from a private plate.

Wight, $10.00 per vol.

144 DRAKE, SAMUEL G. [The Same.]
Thick Royal 8*vo, cloth, bevelled, gilt top, uncut.*
Boston, 1856

Fowle, $16.

145 Drake, Samuel G. Old Indian Chronicle; being a Collection of Exceeding Rare Tracts Written and Published in the Time of King Philip's War, by Persons Residing in the Country; to which are now added Marginal Notes and Chronicles of the Indians from the Discovery of America to the Present Time. *Maps and plates.* 12*mo, cloth.* Boston, 1836

But few printed, scarce.
Fisher, $2.25.

146 Drayton, John. Memoirs of the American Revolution, from its Commencement to the Year 1776, inclusive; as Relating to the State of South Carolina, and Occasionally referring to the States of North Carolina and Georgia. *Fine Portrait, and Plan of the Attack on Fort Moultrie, June,* 1776. 2 *vols.,* 8*vo, boards, uncut, rough edges.* Charleston, 1821

Morrell, $11.00 per vol.; Fisher, half morocco, $8.00 per vol.

147 Duer, William A. Reminiscences of An Old Yorker. By the late William A. Duer, LL.D., President of Columbia College, etc. *Imperial* 8*vo., cloth, uncut.* New York, 1867

Privately Printed for W. L. Andrews, Esq. Only 35 Copies.
These Articles on Old New York originally appeared in the "American Mail," 1847, *and have become so scarce that but one copy could be obtained, from which to reprint this rare volume.*

148 Dunlap, William. History of the Rise and Progress of the Arts of Design in the United States. *Portraits of Dunlap and Gilbert Stuart inserted.* 2 *vols.,* 8*vo, boards. Very scarce.* New York, 1834

Fine, clean copy, in nearly uncut condition.
Wight, half morocco, extra plates, $25 per vol.
Morrell, extended to 4 vols., half morocco, extra plates, $20.00 per vol.; Fisher, half morocco, $10.50 per vol.

149 Dwight, Theodore. History of the Hartford Convention; with a Review of the Policy of the United States Gov-

ernment, which led to the War of 1812. *Portrait of President Madison inserted.* 8*vo, boards.*

New York, 1833

Wight, $2.25.

EARLY VOYAGES UP AND DOWN THE MISSISSIPPI, by Cavalier, St. Cosme, Le Sueur, Gravier, and Guignes. With an Introduction, Notes, and Index. By John Gilmary Shea. *Small* 4*to, uncut.*

Albany, 1861

MUNSELL'S HISTORICAL SERIES, No. 8.
Fowle, half morocco, $27.50.

151 EASTON, JOHN. Narrative of the Causes which led to *Philip's Indian War* of 1675 and 1676. By John Easton, of Rhode Island. With other Documents Concerning this Event, in the Office of the Secretary of State of New York. Prepared from the Originals, with an Introduction and Notes. By Franklin B. Hough. *Map and fac similes. Portrait of King Philip inserted.* 4*to, half morocco, gilt top, uncut.*

Albany, Munsell, 1858

MUNSELL'S HISTORICAL SERIES, No. 2.
LARGE PAPER ; *only* 10 *copies printed ; very rare.*
Fowle, small paper, uncut, $70 ; Fisher, small paper, half morocco, uncut, $50 ; Wight, small paper, half Russia, uncut, $20.

152 EATON, JOHN HENRY. Life of Andrew Jackson, Major-General in the Service of the United States ; Comprising a History of the War in the South, from the Commencement of the Creek Campaign to the Termination of Hostilities before New Orleans. *Portrait.* 8*vo, boards, uncut, rough edges.*

Philadelphia, 1824

2 *Portraits and Autograph of General Jackson Frank, and superscription of letter to John H. Eaton, his Biographer, inserted.*

153 ECHO, THE. With other Poems. *Written by Alsop, Dwight, Cogswell, Hopkins and Trumbull.. Plates after Paintings by Tisdale.* 8*vo, calf.* Phila. 1807

Fisher, uncut, with MSS. of Alsop, $11; Wright, uncut, $4.25.

154 EDWARDS, Rev. JONATHAN. Faithful Narrative of the Surprising Work of God in the *Conversion* of Many *Hundred Souls* in *Northampton* and the neighboring Towns and Villages of *New Hampshire*, in *New England.* In a letter to the *Rev. Dr. Benjamin Coleman, of Boston*, with a Large Preface, etc. *Small* 8*vo, calf.* London, 1738

155 ENGLISH LIBERTIES; or, the Free-born Subjects' Inheritance. Containing *Magna Charta, Charta de Foresta*, the *Habeas Corpus* Act, and several other statutes, with Comments on each of them. Likewise the Proceedings in Appeals of Murder, etc. Compiled first by HENRY CARE, and continued, with large additions, by W. N., of the *Middle Temple*, Esq. *Small* 8*vo., pp.* 288. *Full crimson levant morocco, rich gilt back, and inside borders, gilt edges, by Matthews.*

Boston: Printed by *J. Franklin*, for *N. Buttelph, B. Eliot* and *D. Henchman*, and sold at their shops, 1721

Rare specimen of J. FRANKLIN'S *printing.*

156 ENTICK Rev. JOHN. General History of the Late Wars in Europe, Asia, Africa and America; with Accurate Descriptions of the Battles by Sea and Land. *Portraits, Plans, Maps and Charts.* 5 *vols.* 8*vo, calf.* *Fine copy.* London, 1765

Portraits of Generals Wolfe, Monckton, Lord Howe, etc.

157 EVANS, LEWIS. A Letter *Representing* the Impropriety of Sending Forces to *Virginia*; the Importance of Taking *Frontenac*; and that the Preservation of *Oswego* was owing to General *Shirley's* proceeding thither.

Containing Objections to those parts of *Evan's* General Map and Analysis, which relate to the *French* title to the Country on the North-West side of the *St. Lawrence* River, between Fort *Frontenac* and Montreal, etc. Published in the *New York Mercury*, No. 178, Jan. 5, 1756. With an ANSWER to so much thereof as concerns the public; and the several articles set in a just light. *4to, pp.* 135, *half morocco,* London, 1756

Excessively rare.

Title page written on; otherwise a fine, large copy. Forms No. 2, of a Proposed Series of " Geographical, Historical, Political, Philosophical and Mechanical Essays."

158 EVANS, NATHANIEL. Poems on Several Occasions, with some other Compositions. *8vo, sheep. Fine copy.*
Philadelphia: John Dunlap, 1772

Presentation copy to Lord Balgonie, from DR. BENJAMIN RUSH [*signer of the Declaration of Independence*], *with his signature, and several lines in his autograph.*

Among the subscribers to this rare volume of early American Poetry were Gov. Franklin, of New Jersey; Governor Eden, of Maryland; Hugh Gaine, Joseph Galloway, Dr. Duché, Gen. Wayne, Wm. Paca, etc.

Wight, $5.00; Fisher, $4.50.

FALCKNER, JUSTUS. Grondlycke Onderricht van Sekere Voorname Hoofdstrucken, der Waren, Lontern, Saligmakenden, CHRISTELYCKEN LEERE, Gegrondet op den Grondt van de Apostelen en Propheten, daer JESUS CHRISTUS de Hoecksteen. Is, Angewesen in eenvoudige, dog stigtlycke *Vragen* en *Antwoorden*, door JUSTUS FALCKNER, *Saxe-Germanus*, Minister der Christelycken Protestantsen Genaemten, Lutherfchen Gemcente te *N. York* en *Albanien* ,etc. *Small 8vo., pp.* 128, *original sheep binding.* Gedruckt in Nieuw-York, by
W. Bradfordt, 1708

Fine and very early specimen of William Bradford's printing; excessively rare.

160 FARNHAM, LUTHER. A Glance at Private Libraries. *Plate inserted.* 8*vo.* Boston, 1855

Contains Accounts of the Libraries of Edward Everett, W. H. Prescott, Rufus Choate, etc., etc.

161 FEDERALIST, THE. A Collection of Essays written in fa-favor of the New Constitution, as agreed upon by the Federal Convention, September 17, 1787. 2 *vols.*, 12*mo*, *full crimson levant morocco, gilt back and edges, by Matthews.* New York, 1788

FIRST EDITION; *excessively rare.*
Morrell, boards, uncut, $16.00 per vol.; Roche, boards, uncut, $15.00 per vol.

162 FEDERALIST, THE. A Collection of Essays written in Favor of the New Constitution, as Agreed upon by the Federal Convention, September 17,1787. Reprinted from the ORIGINAL TEXT, with an Historical Introduction and and Notes by H. B. Dawson. *Portrait of Alexander Hamilton on India paper. Imperial* 8*vo*, *cloth, uncut. Vol. I.* Morrisania, N. Y., 1864

LARGE PAPER; ONLY 250 COPIES PRINTED. *Vol. II. is not yet published.*
Morrell, $5.50.

163 FELLOWS, JOHN. The Veil Removed; or, Reflections on David Humphrey's Essay on the Life of Israel Putnam, etc. *Proof Portrait of Gen. Putnam inserted.* 12*mo*, *cloth.* New York, 1843

164 FILSON, JOHN. Discovery, Settlement, and Present State of KENTUCKY, and an Introduction to the Topography and Natural History of that rich and important country; also, Colonel Daniel Boone's Narrative of the Wars in Kentucky, with an Account of the INDIAN NATIONS within the Limits of the United States, their Manners, Customs, Religion, and their Origin. *Portrait of Daniel Boone inserted.* 8*vo*, *full crushed crim-*

son levant morocco, gilt back, edges, and inside borders, by Bedford London, 1793

Fine copy, but wants Map.

165 FINDLEY, WILLIAM. History of the Insurrection in the Four Western Counties of Pennsylvania in the year MDCCXCIV.; with a Recital of the Circumstances Specially Connected therewith; and an Historical Review of the Previous Situation of the Country. 8vo, *boards, uncut, rough edges.* Philadelphia, 1796 12.00

In beautiful condition, and one of the finest copies ever offered for sale. Very rare. Portrait of Washington inserted.

Morrell, half mor., uncut, $19.00; Roche, $14.25, Fisher, half russia, $12.50.

166 FORREST. Catalogue of the Library of Edwin Forrest. Compiled by Joseph Sabin. *Fine Portrait.* 8vo., *uncut.* Philadelphia, 1863 3 50

175 *Copies printed for private distribution; scarce.*

167 FOUNDERS OF NEW ENGLAND. Result of some Researches Among the British Archives for Information Relative to the Founders of New England; Made in the Years 1858, 1859, and 1860. Originally collected for the New England Historic and Genealogical Register, and now corrected and enlarged. By Samuel G. Drake. Third Edition. *Portraits and Map of New England. Rubricated Title.* 4to, *uncut.* Boston, W. E. Woodward, 1865 4 50

LARGE PAPER; 75 *copies printed.*
Contains the very rare portrait of Samuel G. Drake, from private plate.

168 FOWLE. Catalogue of the Choice Collection of Books belonging to William F. Fowle, Esq., of Boston, Mass. *Royal* 8vo, *uncut. Printed on heavy paper.* Cambridge: Printed at the Riverside Press, 1865 1 75

LARGE PAPER: 85 *copies printed.*
Roche, $5.25.

169 Fox, Ebenezer. Revolutionary Adventures of, of Roxbury, Massachusetts. *Portrait; 12mo, cloth.* Boston, 1838

Fisher, half morocco, $2.25.

170 Fox, Ebenezer. Adventures of, in the Revolutionary War. *Illustrated by Elegant* (?) *Engravings from Original Designs. Portrait and plates. 12mo, cloth.* Boston, 1847

171 Franklin, Benjamin. Works, containing several Political and Historical Tracts not included in any former edition, and many Letters, Official and Private, not hitherto published. With Notes and Life, by Jared Sparks. *Portraits and Plates. 10 vols. imperial octavo, cloth, uncut.* Boston, 1840

Large Paper; very scarce.
Fine copy, free from stains.

Fowle, treed calf, $25 per vol.; Bruce, half Russia, $11.50 per vol.; Whitmore, $8 per vol.; Roche, $6.25 per vol.

172 Franklin. Letters to Benjamin Franklin from his Family and Friends, 1751-1790. *Portraits of Mrs. Franklin and Mrs. Bache, with the excessively rare Portrait of Franklin, with fur cap and spectacles, designed by Cochin, 1777, original impression, inserted. 4to, half Russia, gilt top, uncut.* New York, 1859

Large Paper; 10 copies only printed. *Very scarce.*
Morrell, extra plates, $28.

173 Franklin. Letters to Benjamin Franklin, from his Family and Friends, 1751-1790. *With Portraits of Mrs. Franklin and Mrs. Bache. Royal 8vo., paper, uncut.* New York, 1859

Edition limited to 250 copies in Royal 8vo., and 10 on large paper in 4to. A few plates inserted.

Fowle, half morocco, $18; Wight, half Russia, $7.75; Fisher, half morocco, $5.50; Morrell, half morocco, $5.

174 Franklin. The Way to Wealth. Written by the late

Dr. Franklin. Extracted from his Poetical Works. *Portrait ;* 12mo, *uncut ; chapbook.* Nottingham, n. d.

175 Franklin. Familiar Letters and Miscellaneous Papers of Benjamin Franklin; now for the first time published. Edited by Jared Sparks. With Explanatory Notes. *Portrait inserted. Cr.,* 8*vo., bds., uncut.* London, 1833

176 Franklin. Life of Dr. Benjamin Franklin, Written by Himself; with Essays, Humorous, Moral, and Literary. *Portrait ;* 16*mo., sheep.* Boston, 1815

177 Franklin. Memoirs of the Life and Writings of Benjamin Franklin, LL.D., F.R.S., etc., Minister Plenipotentiary from the United States of America, at the Court of France, etc, etc. Written by Himself to a late Period, and Continued to the Time of His Death by His Grandson, William Temple Franklin. Now first published from the Original MSS., etc. *Fine Portrait, engraved by Pye, and fac-simile ; rare Portrait inserted.* 2 *vols.,* 4*to, boards, uncut, rough edges.* London, 1817-1818

178 Fraser, Charles. Reminiscences of Charleston, lately published in the *Charleston Courier*, and now revised and enlarged by the author. 14 *plates inserted, including rare View of Charleston.* 8*vo., half morocco, gilt top.* Charleston, 1854

Privately printed.
Morrell, cloth, $4; Whitmore, cloth, $3.50.

179 Freneau, Philip. Miscellaneous Works, containing his Essays, and Additional Poems. 12*mo, pp.* 429 *; green morocco, gilt ; scarce.* Philadelphia, 1788

Wight, half morocco, uncut, $8.25.

180 Freneau, Philip. Poems Written Between the Years 1768 and 1794. A New Edition, revised and corrected

by the Author, including a considerable number of pieces never before published. *Portrait and Autograph of the Author inserted.* 8*vo*, *green morocco*, *gilt back and edges*, *by Matthews*. *Scarce.*

Monmouth, N. J., 1795

Bruce, half morocco, $9 ; Morrell, half morocco, $8.50.

181 FROTHINGHAM, JR. RICHARD. History of the Siege of Boston, and of the Battles of Lexington, Concord, and Bunker Hill. Also an Account of Bunker Hill Monument, with Illustrative Documents. *Maps and engravings*, 8*vo.*, *cloth.* Boston, 1849

Bruce, $5.50 ; Morrell, $4.25.

182 FROTHINGHAM, JR., RICHARD. The Command in the Battle of Bunker Hill, with a Reply to " Remarks on Frothingham's History of the Battle, by S. Swett." 8*vo.*

Boston, 1850

183 FULLER, THOMAS. Good Thoughts in Bad Times, and Other Papers. *Portrait on India paper.* 8*vo.* ; *full purple crushed levant morocco, rich gilt back and sides, with inside borders, gilt top, uncut, by Matthews.*

Boston, 1863

LARGE PAPER ; *only* 30 *copies printed* ; *very rare.*
Fowle, $10.50.

184 FULTON. Original Autograph Letters of ROBERT FULTON, relative to his Steamboat Enterprise.

1 To Mr. Delacy, New York, October 19, 1812, 1 *p.* 4*to.*
2 " " " November 27, 1812, 1 *p.*, 4*to.*
3 " " " July 24, 1813, 7 *pp.*, 4*to.*
4 " " " November 25, 1813, 3 *pp.*, 4*to.*

With plans of his Steamboat. This valuable Letter is slightly water stained. Portraits of Fulton, etc. Neatly mounted ; 4*to*, *full brown levant morocco, gilt edges.*

Collected and arranged, New York, 1868

UNIQUE.
Morrell, $3.25 ; Bruce, $2.75.

185 FURMAN, GABRIEL. Notes, Geographical and Historical, Relating to the Town of Brooklyn, Long Island, with Notes, and a Memoir of the Author. *4to, uncut.*
Brooklyn : Reprinted for the Faust Club, 1865

Only 120 *copies.*
Morrell, $3.25; Bruce, $2.75.

186 FANNING, COLONEL DAVID. Narrative of, (A Tory in the Revolutionary War with Great Britain); Giving an Account of His Adventures in North Carolina from 1775 to 1783, as Written by Himself. With an Introduction and Explanatory Notes. *Royal 8vo., uncut.*
Richmond, Va. : Printed for Private Distribution only, 1861.
New York, J. Sabin, 1865

LARGE PAPER; 50 *copies reprinted.*

187 FELTMAN, LIEUT. WILLLIAM. Journal of, of the First Pennsylvania Regiment, 1781-82. Including the March into Virginia, and the Siege of Yorktown. *Engraving of the Surrender of Cornwallis inserted.* 8*vo., boards, uncut.* Philadelphia, 1853

GAGE, THOS. New Survey of the West Indies, Containing A Journal of Three Thousand and Three Hundred Miles Within the Mainland of AMERICA, etc., etc. With a Grammar or some few Rudiments of the *Indian* Tongue, etc. *Folio, full green morocco, gilt edges. Original Edition.* London, 1648

"This work appears to have been much celebrated in its time, having been frequently reprinted, and translated into French, Dutch, German, etc."—*Rich.*

189 [GALLOWAY, JOSEPH.] Letters to a Nobleman, on the Conduct of the War in the Middle Colonies. *Plan of the Operations of the British and Rebel Army in the Campaign,* 1777. 8*vo., pp.* 101, *half green morocco.*
London, 1779

"Mr. Galloway was a member of Congress (and Speaker of the House of Assembly of Pennsylvania); he went over to the Royal Army in December, 1776, and continued with it till the evacuation of Philadelphia, in June, 1778, abandoning his estate and property to the value of above forty thousand pounds sterling."

GALLOWAY. Examination of Joseph Galloway, Esq. *See Trials.*

190 GARDEN, ALEXANDER. Anecdotes of the Revolutionary War in America, with Sketches of Character of Persons the most distinguished, in the Southern States, for Civil and Military Services. 8*vo.*, *boards, uncut, rough edges.* Charleston, 1822

Fine, clean copy; rare.

Wight, $19; Morrell, $15; Fisher, half morocco, uncut, $14; Whitmore, half morocco, uncut, $10; Roche, $8.50; Bruce, half morocco, uncut, $8.

191 GARDEN, ALEXANDER. Anecdotes of the American Revolution, Illustrative of the Talents and Virtues of the Heroes and Patriots who acted the most Conspicuous Parts Therein. Second Series. 12*mo*, *boards, uncut, rough edges.* Charleston, 1828

Fine, clean copy; rare.

Wight, $16.50; Fisher, half morocco, uncut, $14: Morrell, $12; Whitmore, $10; Roche, $8.50; Bruce, half morocco, uncut, $8.

The above copies of the very scarce original editions of "Garden's Anecdotes" are in unusual fine condition, being without a blemish.

192 GARRARD, LEWIS H. Chambersburg in the Colony, and the Revolution. A Sketch. 8*vo.*, *cloth.* Philadelphia, 1856

193 GILPIN, THOMAS. Exiles in Virginia; with Observations on the Conduct of the Society of Friends During the Revolutionary War, Comprising the Official Papers of the Government Relating to that Period, 1777-1778. *Fac similes.*

Philadelphia: Printed for the Subscribers, 1848

LIMITED EDITION.

Fisher, extra plates, $9.50; Wight, half morocco, uncut, $7.25; Morrell, autograph letter inserted, $5.50.

194 GLORIOUS PROGRESS OF THE GOSPEL AMONGST THE INDIANS IN NEW ENGLAND. Manifested by Three Letters, under the Hand of that Famous Instrument of the Lord, Mr. JOHN ELIOT, and another from Mr. *Thomas Mayhew*, jun.; both Preachers of the Word, as well to the *English* as *Indians* in *New England;* Wherein the Riches of God's Grace, in the Effectual Calling of Many of Them, is Cleared Up, etc. *Published by Edward Winslow. Small* 4*to, pp.* 28, *polished calf. Scarce.*
London, 1649

195 GORDON, WILLIAM. History of the Rise, Progress, and Establishment of the Independence of the United States of America; Including an Account of the Late War; and of the Thirteen Colonies, from their Origin to that Period. *Maps.* 4 *vols.*, 8*vo, half maroon calf.*
London: Printed for the Author. 1788

Fine, clean copy, almost uncut.

Portraits of Washington, Franklin, Lafayette, and Lord Cornwallis inserted, facing the title page of each volume.

Wight, uncut, $6 per vol.; Bruce, half morocco, uncut, $5.50 per vol.; Morrell, with Portrait of Gordon, $5 per vol.; Roche, uncut, $4 per vol.

196 GRAHAM, GENERAL. Memoir of, with Notices of the Campaigns in which he was engaged from 1779 to 1801. Edited by his Son, Colonel James J. Graham. *Portrait, Plates, and Plan of Yorktown,* 1781. *Rare Portrait of Capt. Asgill inserted. Crown* 8*vo., cloth, uncut.*
Edinburgh, 1862

PRIVATELY PRINTED.

Contains a graphic Account of the romantic and tragic incidents connected with Captain Charles Asgill during the American Revolution. But few copies of this work were printed, and those only for private circulation among the friends and relatives of the family. See Preface.

Morrell, $18; Roche, $8.50.

197 GRANT, MRS. Memoirs of an American Lady; with Sketches

of Manners and Scenery in America, as they existed previous to the Revolution. Second edition. *Fine Autograph Letter, 2 pp., 4to, July 7, 1831, of the Authoress inserted. 2 vols., cr., 8vo, half calf.* London, 1809

198 GRANT, MRS. Memoirs and Correspondence of, of Laggan; 3 *vols.* Also, LETTERS FROM THE MOUNTAINS; 2 *vols.* Edited by her Son, J. P. Grant, Esq. *Fine Portrait. Together, 5 vols, cr., 8vo, cloth, uncut.*

London, 1845

Mrs. Grant passed her early days in the Family of Gen. Schuyler at Albany.

199 GRAHAME, JAMES. History of the United States of North America, from the Plantation of the British Colonies till their Revolt and Declaration of Independence. 4 *vols., 8vo, cloth, uncut.* London, 1836

Fisher, $1.50 per vol.

200 GRAVES, W. Two Letters from W. Graves, Esq., Respecting the Conduct of Rear-Admiral Thomas Graves in North America, during his Accidental Command there for Four Months in 1781. *Plan of the Sea Fight between Admiral Graves and Count De Grasse. Fine Portraits of Admiral Graves and Count De Grasse inserted. 4to, full morocco, gilt back, and richly tooled inside borders, by Matthews.* London, 1782

Original edition, very rare.

201 GRAVES, WILLIAM. Two Letters Respecting the Conduct of Rear-Admiral Graves on the Coast of the United States, July to November, 1781. *4to, uncut.*

Morrisania, N. Y., 1865

Only 100 *copies re-printed.*
Fisher, $1.88.

202 GRAYDON, ALEXANDER. Memoirs of a Life chiefly passed

in Pennsylvania within the last Sixty Years; with Occasional Remarks upon the General Occurrences, Character, and Spirit of that Eventful Period. *Newspaper cuttings inserted.* 12*mo, half Russia, gilt.* Harrisburgh, 1811

203 GRAYDON, ALEXANDER. [The Same.] 12*mo, boards, uncut, rough edges. Scarce in this condition.* Harrisburgh, 1811

204 GREENWOOD ILLUSTRATED. In a Series of PICTURESQUE and MONUMENTAL Views, in highly finished Line Engraving. From Drawings taken on the Spot, by *James Smillie;* the Literary Department by *N. Cleaveland. Beautiful steel plates;* 14 *parts, as originally published; folio.* New York, 1846

LARGE PAPER. *Very scarce.*
Published by Subscription only.

205 GARDEN, ALEXANDER. Anecdote of American Revolution, Illustrative of the Talents and Virtues of the Heroes of the Revolution who acted the most conspicuous parts therein. *Fine Portraits of Lord Cornwallis, and Lord Rawdon inserted.* 3 *vols., folio, uncut.* Brooklyn, 1865

LARGE PAPER; 30 *copies printed.*
Reprinted from the rare originals, with additional matter, by Mr. T. W. Field.

HEWAT, ALEXANDER. An Historical Account of the Rise and Progress of the Colonies of *South Carolina* and *Georgia.* 2 *vols.,* 8*vo, boards, uncut, rough edges. Fine, clean copy; very rare.* London, 1779

Bruce, $6.25 per vol. Roche, calf, $4.00 per vol.

207 HISTORICAL MAGAZINE, and Notes and Queries concerning the Antiquities, History, and Biography of America. *Plates. Vols.* 1 *to* 7, *cloth,* 8, 9, 10 *and* 11, *in numbers,*

7

uncut. Together 11 *vols., small,* 4*to. Scarce.*
Boston and New York, 1857–'67

Volume 10 *wants No.* 11, *volume* 11 *wants Nos.* 4 *and* 11. (*November number.*)

208 HISTORY OF THE DISCOVERIES AND SETTLEMENTS OF THE ENGLISH IN NORTH AMERICA AND THE WEST INDIES. *Multum in Parvo. Small* 8*vo., calf.* Glasgow, 1764

209 HAKLUYT, RICHARD. The principall Navigations, Voiages and Discoueries of the English Nation, made by Sea or ouer Land to the most remote and farthest distant quarters of the earth, at any time within the compasse of these 1500 yeeres: Deuided into three seural parts, according to the positions of the Regions whereunto they were directed, etc. Including the English valiant attempts in searching almost all the corners of the vaste and new world of *America*, etc., etc. BLACKLETTER. *Curious Initial Letters, Head and Tail Pieces, etc. Folio, full calf antique, gilt edges. Very rare.*
Imprinted at London by *George Bishop* and *Ralph Newberie*, Deputies to Christopher Barker, printer to the Queenes most excellent Majestie. 1589

Title page mounted, otherwise a fine copy, containing the six inserted leaves between pages 643 *and* 644, *with account of Sir Francis Drake's voyage to the south.*

210 HAKLUYT. Discovery and conquest of Terra Florida, by Don Ferdinand De Soto, and six hundred Spaniards, his followers, written by a gentleman of Elvas, and translated out of Portuguese, by Richard Hakeluyt. Reprinted from the edition of 1611, with Notes and an Introduction by William B. Rye. *Map,* 8*vo, cloth, uncut.*
London; Printed for the Hakluyt Society, 1851

211 [HALES, S.] History of the United States, from their First

Settlement as Colonies to the close of the War with Great Britain, in 1815. *8vo., pp.* 467, *boards, uncut.* London, 1682

212 HALIBURTON, THOMAS C. An Historical and Statistical Account of Nova Scotia. *Maps, etc.* 2 *vols.*, 8*vo.*, *boards, uncut.* Halifax, 1829

Fisher, half mor., $2.75 per vol.

213 HALLECK, FITZ-GREENE. Fanny: a Poem. With Notes. *Proof Portrait on India Paper, of Halleck, engraved by Burt after miniature by Rogers. Printed entirely on India Paper on one side only. Imperial* 4*to., pp.* 84, *cloth, uncut. Very rare.* ONLY 5 COPIES PRINTED ON INDIA PAPER. New York, 1866

PRIVATELY PRINTED FOR MR. W. L. ANDREWS.

214 HALLECK. Duyckinck, Evart A. Fitz-Greene Halleck. From *Putnam's Magazine*, February, 1868. *Fine Proof Portrait, with* 2 *additional ones inserted.* 4*to., uncut.* New York, 1868.

50 COPIES PRIVATELY PRINTED FOR MR. W. L. ANDREWS.

215 HAMILTON. Coleman, William. A Collection of the Facts and Documents relative to the Death of MAJOR GENERAL ALEXANDER HAMILTON, with Comments: Together with the various Orations, Sermons and Eulogies that have been Published or Written on his life and Character. 16 *Plates inserted, comprising portraits of Hamilton, Burr, Governeur Morris, Dr. Hosack, Gen. Schuyler, Dr. Nott, Mrs. Hamilton*, etc., *together with original autograph note of Col. Aaron Burr.* 8*vo*, *Full brown morocco, gilt. Very rare.*

New York, 1804

Allan, extra plates, $25. Wight, extra plates, $21.

216 HAMILTON. Works of Alexander Hamilton: comprising his most important Official Reports; an improved edition of the Federalist, etc., etc. *Fine Portraits of Hamilton, Jay, and Madison, the latter slightly spotted.* 3 *vols.*, 8*vo*, *calf.* New York, 1810

Roche, half Russia, uncut, $2.12½ per vol.

217 HAMILTON. Hamilton, John C. Life of Alexander Hamilton. By his Son. *Fine Portrait, engraved by Durand, with extra one inserted.* 2 *vols.*, 8*vo*, *cloth*, *uncut.* New York, 1840 41

Fine, clean copy; scarce.
Morrell, $5.75 per vol.; Whitmore, $5.50 per vol.; Roche, $3.50 per vol.

218 HAMILTON CLUB SERIES:

No. I. Life of Alexander Hamilton, by John Williams (*Anthony Pasquin.*)

II. Observations on Certain Documents in the "History of the United States for the Year 1796," by Alexander Hamilton ("*Reynold's Pamphlet*").

III. The Hamiltoniad, by John Williams (*Anthony Pasquin*).

IV. Letters to Alexander Hamilton, King of the Feds. Cidevant Secretary of the Treasury, etc., by Tom Callender. 4 vols., 4to, uncut. New York, 1866

LARGE PAPER; *only* 20 *copies.*

219 HAMILTON, SCHUYLER. History of the National Flag of the United States of America. UNIQUE COPY. *Every leaf has been beautifully inlaid, and extended to quarto size, borders being ruled with red ink, and has* 69 *inserted Plates, comprising rare and curious Portraits of Washington, Putnam, Reed, Arnold, Gage, Franklin, Paul Jones, Commodore Hopkins, etc. Also a great variety of beautifully colored Flags, and the very*

rare Engravings, from the old Columbian Magazine, of the "ARMS," *and the* "GREAT SEAL" *of the United States. Inserted in this volume are also Engravings of* "*Washington's Coat of Arms,*" *and the* "*Military Costume of the Revolution,*" *illuminated in gold and colors. Many of the Illustrations are proofs on India paper. Full rich green levant morocco, back and sides elegantly tooled, gilt edges.* Philadelphia, 1852

220 HAMOR. A Trve Discovrse of the Present Estate of Virginia, and the successe of the affaires there till the 18 of *Iune*, 1614. Together with a Relation of the severall English Townes and Fortes, the assured hopes of that countrie, and the peace *concluded with the Indians.* The Christening of *Powhatans* daughter, *and her marriage with an Englishman.* Written by Raphe Hamor the younger, late Secretarie in that Colony. *Beautiful Portrait of Captain John Smith, printed on folio paper, inserted. Folio, half morocco, gilt top, uncut.*
London, 1615. Albany, 1860

200 COPIES PRIVATELY PRINTED.
Reprinted for Dr. Charles Gorman Barney, of Richmond, Va.
Whitmore, $25.50; Morrell, $14; Roche, $7.

221 HATFIELD AND DEERFIELD. Papers Concerning the Attack on Hatfield and Deerfield by a Party of Indians from Canada, September Nineteenth, 1677. *Map. Royal* 8vo*; full morocco, extra, with inside covers, richly and elaborately tooled, gilt top.*
New York, 1859

PRIVATELY PRINTED: 100 COPIES. *Very rare.*
Club copy; Bradford Club Series, No. 1.
Morrell, $40; Bruce, $27.

222 HAVEN, C. C. Thirty Days in New Jersey Ninety Years Ago: An Essay Revealing New Facts in Connection with Washington and his Army in 1776 and 1777. 8*vo, uncut.* Trenton, 1867

223 Heath, Major-General. Memoirs containing Anecdotes, Details of Skirmishes, Battles, and other Military Events, during the American War. Written by Himself. Published according to Act of Congress. *Portrait of General Heath inserted.* 8vo, *original, sheep binding. Fine, tall copy, scarce.*

Boston, Aug., 1798

In unusually fine condition, being entirely free from stains.

Roche, extra plates, $36 ; Morrell, same copy, $35 ; Whitmore, $7.50

224 Heckewelder, John. Narrative of the Mission of the United Brethren among the Delaware and Mohegan Indians, from its Commencement in the year 1740 to the close of the year 1808. Interspersed with Anecdotes, Historical Facts, Speeches of Indians, and other Interesting Matter, etc. *Portrait.* 8vo, *calf.*

Philadelphia, 1820

Morrell, uncut, $9 ; Roche, uncut, $8.50 ; Bruce, uncut, $5.25 ; Whitmore, uncut, $4.25.

225 Hennepin, Lewis. A New Discovery of a *Vast Country in America*, Extending above Four Thousand Miles, between New France and New Mexico. With a Description of the Great *Lakes*, *Cataracts*, *Rivers*, *Plants and Animals*, etc. With a Continuation : Giving an Account of the Attempts of the *Sieur De la Salle* upon the Mines of *St. Barbe*, etc. The Taking of *Quebec* by the *English ;* with the Advantages of a Shorter Cut to *China* and *Japan*. *Both parts complete. Numerous plates, including the rare view of Niagara Falls.* 8vo, *full rich green crushed levant morocco, gilt back and edges ; inside borders, by Bedford ; very rare.*

London, 1698

Superb copy, tall, and perfectly spotless.

Bruce, half morocco, $18 ; Morrell, calf, $13 ; Fisher, calf, $13.

226 Henry, John Joseph. An Accurate and Interesting Account of the Hardships and Sufferings of that Band of Heroes who traversed the Wilderness in the Campaign against Quebec in 1775. *Rare View of Quebec inserted.* 12*mo*, *sheep*. Lancaster, 1812

Fine, clean copy.
Morrell, $2.50; Bruce, $2.50 ; Fisher, $2.

227 Herbert, Charles. A Relic of the Revolution, containing a full and Particular Account of the Sufferings and Privations of all the American Prisoners captured on the High Seas and carried into Plymouth, England, during the Revolution of 1776, etc. Also, an Account of the several Cruises of the Squadron under the Command of Commodore John Paul Jones, Prizes Taken, etc., etc. *Plates. Portrait of Paul Jones inserted.* 12*mo*, *half morocco, gilt top, by Bradstreet. Scarce.* Boston, 1847

Morrell, $3.25.

228 Hollister, G. H. History of Connecticut, from the First Settlement to the Adoption of the Present Constitution. *Numerous fine steel plates.* 2 *vols.*, 8*vo*, *uncut*, (*sheets folded.*) New Haven, 1855

229 Holm, Thomas Campanius. Description of the *Province of New Sweden*, now called, by the English, Pennsylvania, in America. Compiled from the Relations and Writings of Persons worthy of Credit, and adorned with Maps and Plates. Translated from the Swedish, for the Historical Society of Pennsylvania, with Notes, by Peter S. Du Ponceau, LL.D. *Maps and Plates.* 8*vo*, *boards, uncut, rough edges.* Philadelphia, 1834

Fine, clean copy.

230 Holmes, Abiel. Life of Ezra Styles, D.D., LL.D. A Fellow of the American Philosophical Society, Presi-

dent of Yale College, etc., etc. *Rare Portrait.* 8*vo, calf. Title page stained.* Boston, 1798

Dr. Stiles was the author of the "History of Three of the Judges of King Charles I."

231 HORACE. Lyric Works, translated into English Verse: To which are added a number of Original Poems. By a native of America (*Mr. Parke*). *Curiously Engraved Frontispiece.* 8*vo, calf. Very scarce.*
Philadelphia, 1786

Included in the Original Poems is "VIRGINIA;" *a Pastoral Drama on the Birth-Day of an* ILLUSTRIOUS PERSONAGE, *and the Return of Peace, February* 11*th*, 1784.
Fisher, $3.50.

232 HOW, DAVID. Diary of a Private in Colonel Paul Dudley Sargent's Regiment of the Massachusetts Line, in the Army of the American Revolution. From the Original Manuscript, with Biography, Notes, etc., by George Wingate Chase, and Henry B. Dawson. *Royal* 8*vo, uncut.* Morrisania, N. Y., 1865

250 *copies printed.*

233 HOWE. A Candid and Impartial Narrative of the Transactions of the *Fleet* under the command of *Lord Howe*, from the arrival of the Toulon Squadron, on the Coast of America, to the time of his Lordship's Departure for England, with *Observations.* By an Officer then serving in the Fleet. Second edition, revised and corrected. *Plan of the Situation of the Fleet, within Sandy Hook, mounted on muslin.* 8 *vo, pp.* 58, *boards, uncut, rough edges.* London, 1779

Very scarce.

234 HOWE. The Narrative of Lieutenant-General Sir William Howe relative to His Conduct during His Late Command of the King's Troops in *North America.* To

which are added Some observations upon a Pamphet entitled *Letters to a Nobleman. Portrait of General Howe inserted.* 4*to*, *half green morocco, gilt top. Fine copy* London, 1781

Morrell, $11.

235 HUBBARD, REV. WILLIAM. Narrative of the Indian Wars in New England, from the first Planting thereof in the year 1607 to the year 1677; Containing the Occasion, Rise and Progress of the War with the Indians, etc. 12*mo. Crimson morocco, gilt back and edges, by Matthews.* Worcester, 1801

Scarce.

236 HUBBARD, REV. WILLIAM. History of the Indian Wars in New England from the First Settlement to the Termination of the War with King Phillip, in 1677. *From the original work*, with Historical Preface, Extensive Notes, etc., by Samuel G. Drake. *Map of New England and fac-similes.* 2 *vols., roy.* 8*vo., uncut.* Roxbury, Mass., 1865

LARGE PAPER: 50 *Copies printed.*
Woodward's Historical Series, Nos. 3 *&* 4.

237 HUMPHREYS, DAVID. Miscellaneous Works, (Including Essay on the Life of Putnam.) *Portrait.* 5 *plates inserted.* 8*vo., green morocco, gilt back and edges, by Matthews.* New York, 1804

Presentation copy from Col. Humphreys, with his Autograph.

238 HUTCHINS, THOMAS. A Topographical Description of VIRGINIA, PENNSYLVANIA, MARYLAND, and NORTH CAROLINA, comprehending the Rivers Ohio, Kenhawa, Siota, Cherokee, Wabash, Illinois, Mississippi, etc.; the Climate, Soil, and Produce, whether *Animal, Vegetable,* or *Mineral;* the *Mountains, Creeks, Roads, Distances,*

Latitudes, &c., &c., of every Part laid down in the annexed Map. Published by THOMES HUTCHINS, Captain of the 60th Regiment of Foot, etc., with an APPENDIX containing MR. PATRICK KENNEDY'S Journal up the Illinois River, and a correct list of the different NATIONS and TRIBES of *Indians*, etc. *Plan of the Rapids of the Ohio, Map, etc.*, 8*vo.*, *full green morocco with rich inside borders, gilt top, uncut, by Matthews.*
. London: Printed for the Author, etc., 1778

Very rare.

239 HUTCHINSON, FRANCIS. HISTORICAL ESSAY concerning WITCHCRAFT, with Observations upon Matters of Fact, &c., &c. 8*vo.*, *calf.* London, 1781

Gives an account of the Witchcraft troubles at Salem, Boston and Andover, in New England.

INDIAN HOSTILITIES, 1655. A Brief and True Narrative of the Hostile Conduct of the Barbarous Natives towards the Dutch Nation. Translated by Dr. E. B. O'Callaghan. *Royal* 8*vo*, *hlf. morocco, uncut.*
Munsell, Albany, 1863

ONLY 50 COPIES PRINTED.

241 INDIAN TREATIES. Proceedings of the Commissioners of Indian Affairs appointed by law for the Extinguishment of Indian Titles in the State of New York, with Introduction and Notes by Franklin B. Hough. *Maps.* 2 *vols.*, *small* 4*to cloth, gilt top, uncut.*
Albany, 1861

MUNSELL'S HISTORICAL SERIES, Nos. 9 & 10.
Fowle, hlf. mor. $14 per vol. Whitmore, $5 per vol.

242 IMPARTIAL HISTORY OF THE WAR IN AMERICA, between Great Britain and her Colonies, from its Commencement to the Year 1779. Exhibiting a circumstantial, connected and complete Account of the real *Causes*,

Rise and *Progress* of the *War*, interspersed with Anecdotes and Characters of the different Commanders, and Accounts of such Personages in Congress as have distinguished themselves during the Contest. With an Appendix. Illustrated with a variety of beautiful Copper-Plates, representing real and animated Likenesses of those celebrated Generals who have distinguished themselves in the important contest. *Map, and* 13 *full length portraits of American and British Generals, being those of Generals Washington, Gates, Arnold, Wooster, Putnam, Charles Lee, Com. Hopkins. Samuel Adams, Hancock, Franklin, Gen. Howe, Admiral Howe, American Rifleman.* 8*vo., pp.* 608. *Appendix, pp.* 44. *Boards, uncut.*

Carlisle, 1780

Excesssively rare.
Wight, half calf, $17.

243 INGRAHAM, EDWARD D. Sketch of the Events which preceded the Capture of Washington, by the British, on the twenty-fourth of August, 1814. *Map, with portrait of the Author inserted.* 8*vo, boards, uncut.*

Philadelphia, 1849

PRIVATELY PRINTED.
Presentationn copy from the author, with his own MSS. corrections.
Allan, Autograph Letter inserted, $8. Wight, hlf. mor. Autograph and Portrait inserted, $6.50. Fisher, hlf. mor. $5.50.

244 IRVING, WASHINGTON. History of New York, from the Beginning of the World to the end of the Dutch Dynasty, etc., being the only Authentic History of the Times that ever hath been or ever will be published. By Diedrich Knickerbocker. *Plates, Vignettes, etc., by Allston & Darley. Royal* 8*vo. pp.* 459, *sheets folded.* New York, 1867

LARGE PAPER: *limited edition, beautifully printed.*

Contains the folding plate of "Peter Stuyvesant's army entering New Amsterdam," from a drawing by William Heath of London.

IRVING, WASHINGTON. Life of Washington. *See Washington.*

245 IRVINGIANA. A Memorial of Washington Irving. *Portraits on India Paper, and Fac-simile. 4to, boards, uncut.* New York, 1860

LARGE PAPER: *only* 10 *copies printed.*
Autograph Letter, 2 *pp.,* 8*vo.,* ("*Sunnyside. May* 8, 1857,") *of Irving, inserted, and* 15 *different portraits, proofs on India paper, etc., some rare; also newspaper cuttings.*
Morrell, morocco, extra plates, $65.

JAMAICA. A New History of *Jamaica*, from the Earliest accounts to the taking of *Porto Bello* by Vice-Admiral VERNON, with account of the *Buccaneers, Sir Henry Morgan, Brasiliano, etc.* Second Edition. *Maps.* 8*vo, pp.* 340, *calf.* London, 1740

247 JAY. Treaty of Amity, Commerce and Navigation, between his Britannic Majesty and the United States of America, by their President, etc., Conditionally Ratified on the Part of the United States, at Philadelphia, June 24, 1795, etc. 12*mo, uncut.* Philadelphia, 1795

248 JAY, WILLIAM. Life of John Jay; with Selections from his Correspondence and Miscellaneous Papers. *Portrait.* 2 *vols.,* 8*vo, boards, uncut.* New York, 1833

H. A. Smith, $4 per vol.

249 JEFFERSON, THOMAS. Notes on the State of Virginia. Illustrated with a Map, including the State of Virginia, Maryland, Delaware and Pennsylvania. *Boards, uncut, rough edges.* London, 1787

STOCKDALE'S EDITION. *Fine copy.*
Roche, $7.

250 Jefferson, Thomas. Notes on the State of Virginia. With the Appendix relative to the Murder of Logan's Family. First Hot-pressed Edition. *Fine Portrait of Jefferson, View of the Natural Bridge, and Maps. 8vo, boards, uncut, rough edges.* Philadelphia, 1801

Excessively rare in uncut condition.
Autograph letter, 24 lines, 8vo, of the Author, signed "Th. J.," *inserted.*
Morrell, calf, $5.

251 Johnson, Joseph. Traditions and Reminiscences chiefly of the American Revolution in the South; including Biographical Sketches, Incidents and Anecdotes, few of which have been published, particularly of Residents in the Upper Country. *Maps, Fac-similes, etc., mounted on muslin; curious Portrait of General Moultrie inserted. 8vo, half green morocco, gilt back, gilt top.* Charleston, S. C., 1851

Beautiful copy, very rare.
Though of recent publication, this work is comparatively unknown in Southern collections.
Morrell, cloth, $13. Bruce, half russia, $10.50. H. A. Smith, cloth, $9. Roche, cloth, $8.50

252 Johnson, William. Sketches of the Life and Correspondence of Nathaniel Greene, Major-General of the Armies of the United States, in the War of the Revolution. Compiled chiefly from Original Materials. *Full length Portrait of Gen. Greene, and Maps. 2 vols., 4to, boards, uncut, rough edges.* Charleston, 1822

Rare Contemporary newspaper account of the death of Gen. Greene inserted. Good copy of this work, but as usual somewhat spotted.
Morrell, $12.50 per vol. Whitmore, $11.50 per vol. Fisher, half Russia, $11 per vol. Roche, $7 per vol. H. A. Smith, $5 per vol.

253 Jones, David. Journal of Two Visits made to some Nations of *Indians* on the west side of the River *Ohio*, in the years 1772 and 1773, with a Biographical Notice

of the Author, by Horatio Gates Jones, A. M. *Royal 8vo, uncut.* Burlington, 1774
Reprinted, New York, 1865

LARGE PAPER: *only* 50 *copies.* Sabin's Reprints, No. II.

254 JONES, HUGH. PRESENT STATE OF VIRGINIA, giving a particular and short Account of the *Indian*, *English*, and *Negroe* Inhabitants of that Colony, with a short view of Maryland and North Carolina, &c., &c, *Beautifully printed, with Vignettes and Initial Letters. Royal 8vo, uncut.* London, 1724
Reprinted, New York, 1865

LARGE PAPER; *only* 50 *copies.* Sabin's Reprints, No. V.

255 JONES, JAMES ATHEARN. Traditions of the North American Indians. *Numerous Illustrations in outline, designed and sketched by W. H. Brooks.* 3 *vols., crown 8vo, half calf, gilt. Scarce.* London, 1830

Fisher, hlf. mor., uncut, $7 per vol. H. A. Smith, uncut, $3 per vol.

256 JOSSELYN, JOHN. An Account of Two Voyages to New England. Wherein you have the setting out of a Ship, with the charges; The prices of all necessaries for furnishing a Planter and his Family at his first coming; A Description of the Countrey, Natives and Creatures, with their Merchantil and Physical use; The Government of the Countrey as it is now possessed by the *English*, etc. A large Chronological Table of the most remarkable passages from the first discovering of the Continent of *America* to the Year 1673. By John Josselyn, Gent. *With the plate of the Dragon, frequently wanting. Small 8vo, full panelled calf, red edges.*
London: Printed for Giles Widdows, at the Green-Dragon in St. Paul's Church-yard, 1674

Fine copy of this scarce little book, with good margins.

Roche, $40. Morrell, $32.50. Fisher, $27. Allan, fac-simile title page, $27.

257 JOSSELYN, JOHN. An Account of Two Voyages to New-England, Made during the years 1638–1663. *Medium, 4to, cloth, uncut.* Boston, 1865

75 Copies printed.

258 JOSSELYN, JOHN. New-England's Rarities Discovered in Birds, Beasts, Fishes, Serpents, and Plants of that Country. With an Introduction and Notes by Edward Tuckerman, M.A. *Plates. Medium, 4to, cloth, uncut.* Boston, 1865

75 Copies printed.

259 JOSSELYN, JOHN. [The same].
With an Introduction and Notes by Edward Tuckerman, A.M. *Plates. 8vo, cloth.* Boston, n. d.

Scarce. Presentation copy.

260 JUNIUS. "A LETTER TO AN HONORABLE BRIGADIER GENERAL, Commander-in-Chief of His Majesty's forces in Canada." London, 1760. Now first ascribed to Junius. To which is added, "a Refutation of the Letter, etc. By an Officer," etc. Edited by N. W. Simons, of the British Museum. *Post 8vo, cloth, uncut.*
London, Pickering, 1841

KAPP, FRIEDRICH. Life of Frederick William Von Steuben, Major-General in the Revolutionary Army. With an introduction by George Bancroft. Second edition. *Portrait, with rare additional one inserted. Thick, 8vo, half russia, gilt top, uncut.* New York, 1859

Morrell, $4.75.

262 KEITH, GEORGE. The Presbyterian and Independent Visible CHURCHES in NEW-ENGLAND and elsewhere, brought

to the Test, and examined according to the Doctrine of the Holy Scriptures, in their *Doctrine*, *Ministry*, *Worship*, *Constitution*, *Government*, *Sacraments*, and *Sabbath Day*. More particularly directed to those in *New England*, etc. *Small* 8*vo*, *pp*. 230, *panelled calf*. *Very scarce.* London, 1691

263 KEITH, SIR WILLIAM. HISTORY OF THE BRITISH PLANTATIONS IN AMERICA. With a Chronological ACCOUNT of the most remarkable Things which happened to the first ADVENTURERS in their several Discoveries of that New World. Part I. Containing the History of VIRGINIA; with Remarks on the Trade and Commerce of that Colony. 2 *large folding Maps*. *Small* 4*to*, *pp*. 187. *Full green crushed levant morocco, rich gilt back, and inside borders, gilt edges, by Bedford.* London, 1738

Very Rare.

Splendid copy, perfectly spotless, and with wide margins, of KEITH'S VIRGINIA. *This work was the first of an intended series of* COLONIAL HISTORIES, *but no other ever appeared. Sir William Keith was Governor of Pennsylvania from* 1717 *to* 1726.

Morrell, $22.50.

264 KENNEDY, JOHN P. Discourse on the Life and Character of *George Calvert, the First Lord Baltimore.* Before the Maryland Historical Society, December 9, 1845. 8*vo*. Baltimore, 1845

265 KNIGHT, MADAME. BUCKINGHAM, REV. MR. Journal of, from the Original Manuscripts, written in 1704 and 1710, 12*mo*, *boards*, *uncut*. New York, 1825

Roche, $4.

266 KNIGHT, MADAME. Private Journal of a Journey from Boston to New York in the year 1704, with Introduction and Notes. 4*to*, *uncut*. Albany, 1865

LARGE PAPER; *only* 50 *copies printed.*

267 KNOX, CAPTAIN JOHN. An Historical Journal of the Campaigns in North America, for the Years 1757, 1758, 1759 and 1760: containing the most Remarkable Occurrences of that period, particularly the two *Sieges of Quebec*, etc. *Fine Portraits of Generals Wolfe and Amherst, with Map. 2 vols., 4to calf.*
London: Printed for the Author, 1769

Fine clean copy, very rare.
Whitmore, uncut, $12.00 per vol. Fisher, without plates, $9.50 per vol.

LA FAYETTE. ANDERSON, LEROY. Half an Hour's Amusement at York and James-Town; Preparatory to a Narrative of La Fayette's Return and Reception in Virginia. *Portrait of Lafayette inserted. 8vo, half morocco.*
Richmond, 15th October, 1824

269 LAMB, R. An Original and Authentic Journal of Occurrences during the Late American War, from its Commencement to the year 1783. *8vo., half green morocco, gilt.* Dublin, 1809

Roche, uncut, $5.00; Wight, calf, $4.00.

270 LAMB, R. Memoir of His Own Life. *8vo, half green morocco, gilt.* Dublin, 1811

Morrell, uncut, $5.75.
No Narratives of the exciting period of our Revolutionary War contain so much of interest and novelty as the above two volumes.

271 LAMB, R. An Original and Authentic Journal of Occurrences during the Late American War, from its Commencement to the Year 1783. *8vo, in the numbers as originally published, uncut, rough edges.*
Dublin, 1809

Very scarce in this condition.

272 LAURENS. Materials for History, Printed from Original Manuscripts. With Notes and Illustrations. By

Frank Moore. Correspondence of Henry Laurens, of South Carolina. Illustrated Copy, *having* 38 *plates inserted, consisting of* 10 *rare and beautiful Portraits, all different, of Henry Laurens; also Portraits of Generals Washington, Gates, Sullivan, Moultrie, Hamilton, Cornwallis, Admiral D'Estaing, W. H. Drayton, Tom Paine, Lafayette, Franklin, Duche, etc., etc., together with a fine and interesting Autograph Letter of Laurens.* 5 *pp.*, 4*to*, "*Savannah, May* 10, 1769." 4*to, full crimson levant morocco, gilt back, gilt top, uncut.*

New York: Printed for the Zenger Club, 1861

250 Copies printed.

This volume also contains a beautiful Portrait, on India paper, of Henry Laurens, engraved for the work.

273 Law, William. An extract from a Treatise called, The Spirit of Prayer; or, The Soul Rising out of the Vanity of *Time* into the Riches of *Eternity*, etc. *Small* 8*vo*, *pp.* 47, *half levant morocco, gilt edges.*

Philadelphia: Printed by B. Franklin and D. Hall, 1760

Wight, calf, $10.

274 Lee. Memoirs of the Life of the late Charles Lee, Esq., Second in Command in the Service of the United States of America during the Revolution; to which are added his Political and Military Essays, etc. *Rare full length portrait of Gen. Lee inserted.* 8*vo*, *boards, uncut, rough edges.*

London, 1792

Morrell, $8.00; Roche, $7.00.

275 Lee, Henry. Memoirs of the War in the Southern Department of the United States. *Portraits of General Greene and Lord Cornwallis, engraved by Edwin. Por-*

trait and Autograph Letter of Gen. Lee inserted. 2 *vols.*, 8*vo, boards, uncut, rough edges.*
Fine copy, rare. Philadelphia, 1812

Morrell, extra plates, $18.00 per vol.; Fisher, calf, $7.50 per vol.; Wight, $5.75 per vol.

276 LENDRUM, JOHN. History of the American Revolution, with a Summary View of the State and Character of the British Colonies of North America. New Edition, revised and corected. 2 *vols.*, 12*mo, sheep.*
Exeter, 1836

277 LETTERS BETWEEN THEOPHILUS AND EUGENIO, on the Moral Pravity of Man, and the Means of His Restoration. Wrote in the East Indies, and now First Published from the Original Manuscript. *Small* 4*to, pp. IV.*, 64. *Full morocco, gilt.*
Philadelphia: Printed and Sold by B. Franklin. 1747

In beautiful condition; rare.
Morrell, $15.

278 LETTERS to the Right Honorable the *Earl of Hillsborough*, from *Governor Bernard*, *General Gage*, and the Honorable His Majesty's Council for the Province of MASSACHUSETTS-BAY. With Appendix, etc. *Rare Portrait of General Gage inserted.* 8*vo, pp.* 165, *half green morocco, gilt.* Boston, 1769
London [1769]

279 LEWIS AND CLARK. History of the Expedition under the Command of Captains Lewis and Clark, *to the sources of the Missouri*, thence across the Rocky Mountains and down the River Columbia to the Pacific Ocean Performed during the years 1804–5–6. By order of the Government of the United States. Prepared for the press by Paul Allen, Esq. *Maps. Portrait of Captain Meriwether Lewis inserted.* 2 *vols.*, 8*vo, boards,*

uncut, rough edges. Fine, clean copy. Very rare in this condition. Philadelphia, 1814

Fisher, sheep, $7 per vol.

280 LEWIS AND CLARK. Travels to the source of the *Missouri River* and across the American Continent to the Pacific Ocean, performed by order of the Government of the United States, in the years 1804, '05, and '06. *Full length Portrait of Captain Lewis inserted.* 3 *vols.*, 8*vo, calf, gilt.* London, 1817

Fine copy.
Fisher, half morocco, uncut, $4 per vol. Bruce, $2.50 per vol.

281 LEWIS AND CLARKE. *Travels* to the *Source of the Missouri* River, and across the American Continent to the Pacific Ocean. Performed by order of the Government of the United States, in the Years 1804, 1805 and 1806. *Map.* 4*to, pp.* 663, *boards, uncut, rough edges.* London, 1814

Fine, clean copy, very rare.

282 LEWIS, Gen. ANDREW. The Orderly Book of that Portion of the American Army stationed at or near Williamsburgh, Va., under the command of General Andrew Lewis, from March 18th, 1776 to August 28th, 1776. Printed from the Original Manuscript, with Notes and Introduction, by Charles Campbell, Esq. *Portrait of Gen. Henry Lee inserted. Small* 4*to, half morocco, uncut.* Richmond, Va., 1860

PRIVATELY PRINTED; only 100 copies. *Very Scarce.*
Printed by Joel Munsell, Albany.
Fowle, $47.50; Wight, $15.50; Whitmore, $13.50; Morrell, $10.50

283 LOSKIEL, GEORGE HENRY. History of the Mission of the United Brethren among the Indians in North America. In Three Parts. Translated from the German by

Christian Ignatius La Trobe. *Map.* *8vo, half purple morocco, gilt top, uncut.* London, 1794
Fine copy, scarce.

Wight, $8. H. A. Smith, $7.50. Fisher, calf, $7.50.

284 LOSSING, BENSON J. The Pictorial Field-Book of the Revolution; or, Illustrations by Pen and Pencil, of the History, Biography, Scenery, Relics, and Traditions of the War for Independence. *With several hundred engravings on wood, by Lossing & Barrett, chiefly from Original Sketches by the Author. In* 30 *numbers, as originally published, making* 2 *vols., royal* 8*vo, uncut.* New York, 1850

FIRST EDITION: *excessively rare.*
Morrell, half morocco, uncut, $13.00 per vol.; Whitmore, $8.50 per vol.; Bruce, $7.75 per vol.; Wight, $6.50 per vol.

285 LOUISIANA. BOSSU. Travels through that part of North America formerly called *Louisiana.* Translated from the French by John Reinhold Forster, F.A.S. Illustrated with *Notes* relative chiefly to *Natural History,* etc. 2 *vols.,* 8*vo, calf.*
Fine, tall copy. London, 1775

Fisher, half mor., $3.25 per vol.

286 LOVE AND PATRIOTISM! or, the Extraordinary Adventures of M. DU PORTAIL, late Major General in the Armies of the United States. Interspersed with many surprising incidents in the Life of the late COUNT PULASKI. *Portrait* of *Pulaski inserted. Small* 8*vo, pp.* 59. *Full green levant morocco, gilt back, inside borders and edges by Bedford.* Boston, 1799

Fine copy, very rare.

287 LOVEWELL. The Expeditions of Captain John Lovewell and His Encounters with the Indians; including a Par-

ticular Account of the Pequaket Battle with a History of that Tribe; and a Reprint of Rev Thomas Symmes's Sermon. By Frederic Kidder. *Map, 4to, uncut.*
Boston, 1865

LARGE PAPER ; 25 *copies only printed.*

288 LOWELL, JAMES RUSSELL. Poems. *Royal 8vo, boards, uncut.*

LARGE PAPER : PRIVATELY PRINTED. Cambridge, 1844

Handsomely printed on heavy white paper.

MACK, DOCTOR EBENEZER. The Cat-Fight; a Mock Heroic Poem. Supported with Copious Extracts from Ancient and Modern Classic Authors. *Curious Plates by D. C. Johnston.* 12*mo, boards, uncut.*
New York, 1824

290 MACKENZIE ALEXANDER SLIDELL. Life of Stephen Decatur, a Commodore in the Navy of the United States. *Engraved Title, with Portrait.* 53 *plates inserted, many very fine ; also rare Autograph Letters of Commodores Decatur and Bainbridge.* 8*vo, full green morocco, gilt back, gilt top, uncut, by Matthews.*

LARGE PAPER : *scarce.* Boston, 1846

291 MADISON. The Papers of James Madison, purchased by order of Congress; being his Correspondence and Reports during the Congress of the Confederation and his reports of Debates in the Federal Convention. Now published from the Original Manuscripts, under the Superintendence of Henry D. Gilpin. *Fac-similes. Portrait of Madison inserted.* 3 *vols.*, 8*vo, boards, in almost uncut condition. Excessively rare.*
Washington, 1840

Fine copy, entirely free from stains.
Morrell, $7 per vol. Wight, sheep, $7 per vol. Whitmore, sheep, $6 per vol.

292 MANATI ORE LONG ILE. The Commodities of the Iland called Manati ore Long Ile, which is in the *Continent of Virginia. Map.* 8vo, *half crimson morocco, gilt top, uncut.*

PRIVATELY PRINTED: 50 *copies. Very rare.*
Imprinted by J. M. for J. G. S. *And for sale at the sign of the Two Storks.*
But few copies have the Map.

293 MANTE, THOMAS. The History of the Late War in *North America,* and the Islands of the West Indies, including the Campaigns of MDCCLXIII and MDCCLXIV against his Majesty's Indian Enemies. *Maps wanting, but has inserted an excessively rare contemporary print, brilliant impression, of the "Defeat and Death of Gen. Braddock in North America."* 4*to, pp.* 542, *calf. Fine, clean copy.* London, 1772

On pages 6 *and* 7 *of this very rare work will be found the* ORIGINAL *account from which Irving gives a description of the attempted assassination of Washington by his Indian guide, in* 1753.

294 MARBOIS, M. BARBE. Complot D'Arnold et de Henry Clinton contre les E'tats-Unis D'Amerique et le Général Washington. September 1780. *Fine Portraits of Gens. Washington and Arnold, designed by Du Simitier, and Map.* 8*vo, half purple, levant morocco, gilt top, uncut.* Paris, 1831

LARGE PAPER. *Scarce. Title page repaired.*

295 MARBOIS, M. MARBE. [The same.]
8*vo, uncut.* Paris, 1816

296 MARSH, LUTHER R. General Woodhull and his Monument. An Oration on the Life, Character and Public Services of General Nathaniel Wooodhull, etc. *Plates.* 8*vo.*
New York, 1848

297 MARSHALL, CHRISTOPHER. Passages from the Remem-

brancer of, Member of the Committee of Observation and Inspection, of the Provincial Conference, and of the Council of Safety. Edited by William Duane, Jr. 12*mo, half crimson levant morocco, gilt top, uncut.*

Philadelphia, 1839

298 MASON, MAJOR JOHN. A Brief History of the PEQUOT War; especially of the Memorable *Taking* of their Fort at Mistick, in Connecticut, in 1737. Written by Major John Mason, a principal Actor therein, as then Chief *Captain* and Commander of *Connecticut Forces.* With an *Introduction* and some Explanatory *Notes* by Rev. Mr. Thomas Prince. *Rare plate of "Captain Mason's Engagement with the Indians inserted." Small 8vo, full polished calf, gilt back, edges, and inside borders, by Pratt.*

Boston: Printed and Sold S. KNEELAND & T. GREEN in Queen Street. 1736

Fore edges neatly mended, but text unimpaired, and otherwise a fine, clean copy of this excessively rare work.

Morrell, $51.

299 MASSACHUSETTS HISTORICAL SOCIETY. Proceedings of the, from 1855 to 1865. *Numerous fine steel plates, fac-similes, etc. 6 vols., 8vo, cloth.*

Boston, 1859–1866

Contains the beautiful engraving of WASHINGTON *by* MARSHALL *from* GULLIGHER'S *Painting, also fine portraits of* THOMAS DOWSE, EVERETT, PRESCOTT, *etc., etc.*

300 MATHER COTTON. Magnalia Christi Americana; or, the Ecclesiastical History of New England, From Its First Planting in the Year 1620, unto the Year of our Lord, 1698. In Seven Books. By the Reverend und Learned *Cotton Mather*, M. A. and Pastor of the North Church in *Boston, New-England. Map of New-England and New York. Folio. Full Panelled calf, richly gilt*

back and edges by Bedford. Beautiful specimen of binding. London, 1702

This copy has the leaf of advertisements often wanting, also all the titles, etc.

Inserted in this superb copy of the "Magnalia," is a long ORIGINAL AUTOGRAPH LETTER *of* COTTON MATHER, *over forty lines, folio, and in fine order, signed* "CO. MATHER."

Roche, $50. Corwin, $50. Bruce, $41.50. Wight, $39. Morrell, $38.50. H. A. Smith, $35.

301 MATHER, COTTON. India Christiana. A discourse delivered unto the Commissioners for the propogation of the GOSPEL among the *American* Indians which is Accompanied with several Instruments relating to the Glorious *Design* of Propagating our Holy *Religion* in the *Eastern* as well as the *Western*, INDIES. An Entertainment which they that are *Waiting for the Kingdom of* GOD will receive as *Good News from a far Country. Small 8vo, pp.* 94, *and corrigenda. Original calf binding.*

Boston, in New-England: Printed by B Green, 1771

Fine tall copy; very rare.

302 MATHER, COTTON. The Christian Philosopher: A Collection of the Best Discoveries in Nature, with Religious Improvements. *8vo, calf, pp.* 304. London, 1721

303 MATHER, COTTON. The Wonders of the Invisible World. Being an Account of the Tryals of several Witches lately Executed in New England. To which is added a farther Account of the Tryals of the New England Witches. By Increase Mather, D.D. *Portrait, post 8vo, cloth, uncut.* London, 1862

304 MATHER, INCREASE. Komhtotpaqia; or, A Discourse Concerning Comets; Wherein the Nature of *Blazing Stars* is Enquired Into. With an Historical Account of all the *Comets* which have appeared from the Beginning

of the World unto this present Year, M, DC, LXXXIII. *Expressing* the Place in the Heavens where they were seen ; Their Motion, Forms, Duration ; and the Remarkable Events which have Followed in the World, so far as they have been by Learned Men Observed. As also Two *Sermons* Occasioned by the Late *Blazing Stars.* By *Increase Mather*, Teacher of a Church at *Boston*, in *New England. Rare Autograph Marriage Certificate*, 1706, *and signed by Increase Mather, inserted. Small* 8*vo, full crimson levant morocco, gilt back, with inside borders richly tooled, gilt edges, by Bedford.* BOSTON IN NEW ENGLAND. Printed by S. (amuel) G. (reen) for S. (amuel) S. (ewall), and Sold by *J. Browing*, at the corner of the Prison Lane, next the Town House, 1683

Fine Copy of this excessively rare work, some of the leaves being in proof condition. Has the THREE *title pages—that to the first Sermon, "Heaven's Alarm to the World," bearing date, Boston,* 1682. *Discourse, pp.* 143 ; *"Heaven's Alarm," pp.* 38 ; *"The Latter Sign," pp.* 32.

305 MATHER, INCREASE. Remarkable Providences illustrative of the Earlier Days of American Colonization. With Introductory preface, by George Offer. *Portrait. Post* 8*vo, cloth, uncut.* London, 1856

306 MATHER, INCREASE. History of King Philip's War; also, a History of the same War, by the Rev. Cotton Mather, D.D. With Introduction and Notes by Samuel G. G. Drake, *Portraits, etc. Small* 4*to, sheets folded.* Boston, 1862

250 COPIES PRINTED.
Very scarce in this condition.

307 MATHER. INCREASE. The same, *Small* 4*to, cloth, gilt top, uncut.* Boston, 1862

250 COPIES PRINTED.
Fowle, $16; Fisher, $10.

308 MATHER, INCREASE. Early History of New England;

being a Relation of Hostile Passages between the Indians and European Voyagers and First Settlers; with a full Narrative of Hostilities, to the Close of the War with the Pequots, in the Year 1637, etc., with Introduction and Notes, by Samuel G. Drake. *Small 4to, cloth, gilt top, uncut.* Boston, 1864

250 COPIES PRINTED.
Fowle, $21.

309 MAUDE, JOHN. Visit to the FALLS OF NIAGARA in 1800. *Fine plates, with 22 extra ones inserted, including* 10 *different Views of Niagara Falls, some very rare; also portraits of Washington, Putnam, Major Andre, Colonel Brandt, General Wolfe, etc. The whole book printed entirely on India paper, of which only* FOUR COPIES *were issued in this style.* 8*vo, full green levant morocco, gilt. Very rare.* London, 1826

This edition contains a beautiful Portrait of the Author.

310 M'CALL, CAPTAIN HUGH. History of Georgia, containing Brief Sketches of the most Remarkable Events, up to the present Day. *Portrait of General Oglethorpe inserted.* 2 *vols.,* 8*vo, full polished calf, gilt back and edges, by Pratt.* Savannah, 1811-16
Fine copy, excessively rare.

Morrell, uncut, $21.00 per vol.

311 MILITARY JOURNALS OF TWO PRIVATE SOLDIERS—1758-1775, with numerous Illustrative Notes; to which is added a Supplement, containing Official Papers on the Skirmishes at Lexington and Concord. *Plate,* 8*vo, cloth.* Poughkeepsie, 1855
A limited edition only printed.
Fisher, half mor., $4.25; Morrell, $3.00; Wight, $5.00.

312 MITCHEL, JONATHAN. A Discourse of the GLORY to which GOD hath called BELIEVERS by JESUS CHRIST. Delivered in some SERMONS, etc. Second edition, with a

Preface, by INCREASE MATHER, D.D. *Small* 8*vo*, *pp.* 29, *original sheep binding.* Boston, 1721

In good condition.

313 MITCHILL, SAMUEL LATHAM. Observations Anatomical, Physiological, and Pathological, on the Absorbent Tubes of ANIMAL BODIES. To which are added GEOLOGICAL REMARKS ON THE MARITIME PARTS OF THE STATE OF NEW YORK. 12*mo.* New York, 1787

Excessively Rare. Dr. Mitchill's first publication.

314 MOLL. Atlas Minor; or a SET of Sixty-two New and Correct MAPS, of all Parts of the World. All composed and done by HERMAN MOLL, Geographer. 4*to*, *calf.* London, 1729

Includes Maps of New England, New York, New Jersey, Pennsylvania, Virginia, Maryland, Carolina, etc., etc.

315 MONTHLY MILITARY REPOSITORY. Dedicated to the Military of the United States of America by Charles Smith. Complete. *Curious Portraits of Washington and Wayne, Military Maps, Views, &c., of the most important battles of the Revolution.* 2 *vols.*, 8*vo*, *calf.* New York, 1796

Fine copy. These volumes contain the original issue of the very rare History of "THE AMERICAN WAR, FROM 1775 TO 1783, WITH PLANS," BY CHARLES SMITH, *which was published the following year* (1797) *as a separate volume, a copy of which brought in Morrell's sale* (1866) $25.
Bruce, $5.50 per vol.

316 MOODY, LIEUT. JAMES. NARRATIVE OF HIS EXERTIONS AND SUFFERINGS IN THE CAUSE OF GOVERNMENT, Since the Year 1776; authenticated by proper certificates. *Small* 8*vo*, *pp.* 64, *green moroeco, gilt back and edges, by Matthews.* London, 1783

Fine copy; very *rare.*
"Lieut. Moody, an American farmer, was so harrassed by mobs, associations, and committees, that, driven into the British lines, he

became an active and, in some instances, successful partisan against his countrymen."

Bruce, half morocco, $27.

317 MOODY, LIEUT. JAMES. Narrative of his Exertions and Sufferings in the Cause of the Government since the Year 1776. *Written by Himself*, with the Author's last corrections. Authenticated by proper Certificates. *With an Introduction and Notes by* CHARLES I. BUSHNELL. *Plates. Fine Portraits of Sir Henry Clinton, Rochambeau, Gens. Arnold, Gates, and Wayne inserted.* 8*vo, uncut.* New York, 1865

PRIVATELY PRINTED.

318 MOORE, FRANK. Diary of the American Revolution. From Newspapers and Original Documents. *Portraits and Plates, on India Paper.* 2 *vols, royal* 8*vo, uncut.* New York, 1865.

LARGE PAPER: 100 *copies printed.*

Morrell, $8.50 per vol,

319 MOORE, GEORGE H. "Mr. Lee's Plan—March 29, 1777." The Treason of Charles Lee, Major-General, Second in Command in the American Army of the Revolution *Portraits and fac-similes. Engraving of* "*Washington at Monmouth,*" *after Darley, inserted.* 8*vo, cloth, uncut.* New York, 1860

Fowle, $6.50. Whitmore, $3.25. H. A. Smith, $3.

320 MOORE, HUGH. Memoir of Col. Ethan Allen; containing the most interesting incidents connected with his private and public career. 12*mo, cloth.* Plattsburgh, N. Y., 1834

321 MOORE, SR., M. A. Life of Gen. Edward Lacey, with a List of Battles and Skirmishes in South Carolina, during the Revolutionary War. 8*vo. Scarce.* Spartanburg, S. C., 1859

322 MORRELL. Bibliotheca Americana. Catalogue of the entire Private Library of Mr. T. H. Morrell; comprising a Choice Collection of Books on the History and Antiquities of America, Illustrated Works, etc. To be sold at Auction, November 8th, 9th, & 10th, 1866. *Priced.* 4*to, uncut.* New York, 1866

LARGE PAPER; *only* 10 *copies printed.*

323 MORRELL. Bibliotheca Americana. Catalogue of a Valuable Collection of Books, belonging to Mr. T. H. Morrell; consisting of rare Works on the History and Antiquities of America, Illustrated Volumes, etc. To be Sold at Auction, January 12th and 13th 1869. 4*to., uncut.* New York, 1868

LARGE PAPER; *only* 6 *copies printed.*

324 MORRIS, CAPTAIN THOMAS. Miscellanies in Prose and Verse, (WITH HIS JOURNAL IN AMERICA.) *Fine Portrait.* 8*vo., half morocco, Very scarce.* London, 1791

This rare book contains a graphic account of several incidents in connection with the celebrated "Pontiac War."
Roche, $4.50.

325 MORRIS, GEORGE P. Poems. The Deserted Bride and other Productions. *Portrait, and fine plates, by the best American Engravers, from paintings by* WEIR *and* DARLEY. 8*vo, cloth, gilt. Scarce.* New York, 1853

326 MORSE, JEDIDIAH. Sermon delivered at Charlestown, in the Commonwealth of Massachusetts, February 19, 1795: being the Day Recommended by GEORGE WASHINGTON, President of the United States of America, for *Public Thanksgiving and Prayer.* 8*vo.* Boston, 1795

327 MORSE, JEDIDIAH. Annals of the American Revolution; or a Record of the Causes and Events which produced

and terminated in the Establishment of the American Republic, etc. *Plates, comprising views of the Battle of Saratoga, Capture of Andre, Storming of Stony Point, etc.* 8vo, *half morocco.*
Hartford, 1824

Morrell, autograph inserted, $5. Fisher, $3.50.

328 MORSE, REV. JEDIDIAH. Report of the Secretary of War of the United States, on Indian Affairs, comprising a Tour performed in the Summer of 1820, etc., for the purpose of ascertaining the Actual State of the Indian Tribes in our Country. *Map and Portrait.* 8vo., *bds., uncut, rough edges.* New Haven, 1822

Morrell, $2.

329 MORTON, NATHANIEL. NEW-ENGLAND'S MEMORIAL; or A brief Relation of the most Memorable and Remarkable Passages of the Providence of God, manifested to the Planters of *New-England* in *America;* with special Reference to the first Colony thereof, Called New-Plymouth, &c., &c. Published for the Use and Benefit of present and future Generations, by NATHANIEL MORTON. *Second Edition. Small* 8vo, *Crimson levant morocco, gilt back and edges, by Pratt. Boston: Reprinted for Daniel Hinchman, at the*
Corner Shop over-against the Brick-Meeting-House,
1721

Fine copy.
"The first edition of this work was printed at Cambridge, N. E., in 1669, small 4to. The second edition (the above) appeared in Boston in 1721, with a Supplement by JOSIAH COTTON, Register of Deeds for the county of Plymouth."—*Rich.*

230 MOULTRIE, WILLIAM. Memoirs of the American Revolution, so far as it related to North and South Carolina, and Georgia. Compiled from the most Authentic Materials, the Author's Personal Knowledge of the various Events, and including an Epistolary Correspondence

on Public Affairs, with Civil and Military Officers, at that Period. *Fine Portrait, with extra one inserted.* 2 *vols.*, 8*vo, full blue morocco, gilt, with inside borders, by Bedford.* New York, 1802

Splendid copy ; *excessively rare.*
Fisher, $16.50 per vol. ; Bruce, $10.50 per vol. , Roche, $7.75, per vol.

331 MOURT, G. Mourt's Relation ; or, Journal of the Plantation at Plymouth. With an Introduction and Notes by Henry Martin Dexter. 4*to, uncut.*
Boston, J. K. Wiggin, 1865

LARGE PAPER ; *only* 35 *copies printed.*

332 MURRAY, HUGH. The United States of America ; their History from the Earliest Period ; their Industry, Commerce, National Works, etc., with Illustrations of the Natural History, by James Nicol. *Woodcuts. Post* 8*vo, half calf.* Edinburgh, 1844

333 MURRAY, HUGH. An Historical and Descriptive Account of British America ; comprehending Canada Upper and Lower, Nova-Scotia, New Brunswick, Newfoundland, etc., with Illustrations of the Natural History, by James Wilson, F.R.S., and others. *Map and Woodcuts.* 3 *vols., post* 8*vo, half calf.*
Edinburgh, 1839

334 MURRAY, REV. JAMES. An Impartial History of the Present *War* in *America ;* containing an Account of its Rise and Progress, the Political Springs thereof, with its various Successes and Disappointments, on Both Sides. *Maps and* 22 *Portraits of American and British Officers, brilliant impressions, with very rare portrait of the Author inserted.* 2 *vols.*, 8*vo, calf.*
London, 1778

Fine copy.
The portraits include those of Gens. Washington, Charles Lee, Putnam, Arnold, Gates, Montgomery, Gage, Burgoyne, etc.

335 Murray, Rev. James. Sermons to Asses, to Doctors in Divinity, to Lord's Spiritual, and to Ministers of State, with Original Sketch of the Author's Life. *Portrait.* 8*vo, boards, uncut.* London, 1819

336 Museum of Remarkable and Interesting Events, containing Historical and other Accounts of Adventures, Incidents of Travel and Voyages, Scenes of Peril, and Escapes, Military Achievements, etc., etc.; with a full Account of the Captivity and truly wonderful escape of Thomas Andros from the Old Jersey Prison Ship during the Revolutionary War, written recently by himself. Compiled principally by J. Watts. 25 *Engravings, including representation of "the Escape of Rev. Thomas Andros from the Old Jersey Prison Ship."* 2 *vols.,* 8*vo, half green crushed levant morocco, gilt back and edges. Scarce.*
Cleveland, Ohio, 1844

A few pages very slightly water stained, otherwise a beautiful copy.

337 Munsell's Series of Local History:

1. *Pioneer History of the Champlain Valley;* being an Account of the Settlement of the town of Willsborough, by William Gilliland, together with his Journal and other Papers, and a Memoir, and Historical and Illustrative Notes, by Winslow C. Watson, Esq.
Albany, 1863

2. *Sir Charles Henry Frankland,* Baronet: or, Boston in Colonial Times, by Elias Nason, M.A.
Albany, 1865

3. *Random Recollections of Albany,* 1800 to 1808, by Gorham A. Worth; with Notes. *Numerous portraits and plates, on steel and wood.* Albany, 1866

4. *History of Lake Champlain* from its Exploration by the French in 1609, to the close of the year 1814, by Hon. Peter S. Palmer. *Plans of naval actions.*
Albany, 1866

5. *The Sexagenary ;* or, Recollections of the Revolutionary War, by S. De Witt Bloodgood, Esq. *Portraits of Schuyler, Burgoyne and Lady Harriet Ackland.*
Albany, 1866

6. *Letters and Journals* relating to the War of the American Revolution, and the Capture of the German Troops at Saratoga, by Mrs. General Riedesel ; translated from the original German, by William L. Stone. *Portrait.*
Albany, 1867

7. *Tah-Gah-Jute ;* or, Logan and Cresap, an Historical Essay, by Brantz Mayer. (A Vindication of Captain Cresap against the Charge of Murdering the Family of Logan, etc.) Albany, 1867

8 & 9. *Memoirs and Letters and Journal of Major-General Riedesel,* during his Residence in America. Translated from the Original German of Max von Eelking. By William L. Stone. *Portrait and Plates. 2 vols. In all 9 vols., Royal 8vo, uncut.*

LARGE PAPER. Albany, Munsell, 1863-67

Of No. 1, but 30 copies were printed ; of the others, 50 copies.

338 MUNSELL, JOEL. Typographical Miscellany. *Rare Portrait of Isaiah Thomas inserted. 8vo, cloth.*
Albany, 1850

NANTUCKET. PAPERS relating to the ISLAND of NANTUCKET. With Documents relating to the Original Settlement of that Island, Martha's Vineyard, and other Islands adjacent, known as Duke's County, while under the Colony of New York. Compiled from official Records in the Office of the Secretary of State at Albany, New York. With an Introduction and Notes by Franklin B. Hough. *Map and fac-simile autographs, Small 4to., cloth uncut.* J. Munsell, Albany, 1856

PRIVATELY PRINTED : *and only 150 copies.*

Excessively rare in uncut condition, nearly every copy having been bound for presentation.

Fowle, half calf, trimmed, $40. Roche, half calf, trimmed, $18. Morrell, half morocco, trimmed, $12.

340 NANTUCKET. The same.
Half morocco. Albany, 1856

PRIVATELY PRINTED: 150 *copies. Scarce.*

341 NEAL, DANIEL. History of New-England, Containing an Impartial Account of the Civil and Ecclesiastical Affairs of the Country. To which is added, The Present State of New England, etc. *Map.* 2 *vols.,* 8*vo, panelled calf.* London, 1720

Fine copy.

342 NEILSON, CHARLES. An Original, Compiled and Corrected Account of *Burgoyne's Campaign*, and the Memorable Battle of Bemis's Heights, September 19, and October 7, 1777, from the most authentic sources of Information, etc. *Map,* 12*mo, cloth.* Albany, 1844

Fisher, half morocco, autograph, etc, inserted, $8.

343 NEW-ENGLAND PRIMER, Improved for the more Easy Attaining the True Reading of English. With Mr. Cotton's *Catechism*, etc. *Woodcut portrait of John Hancock.* 16*mo, boards.*
Boston, 1777. Reprint in Fac-simile.

Fisher, $3.25.

344 NEW YORK. Account of the Terrific and Fatal Riot at the Astor Place Opera House, on the night of May 10th, 1849; with the Quarrels of Forrest and Macready, etc., with "THE REPLIES FROM ENGLAND, ETC., to certain Statements circulated in this County respecting MR. MACREADY." *Engraving of the "Scene of the Riot." Portraits of Macready as "Macbeth," Forrest, etc., inserted.* 8*vo, hlf. morocco. Scarce.*
New York, 1849

345 New York. A Rejoinder to "The Replies from England, etc," together with an Impartial History and Review of the Lamentable Occurrences at the Astor Place Opera House, on the 10th of May, 1849. By an American Citizen. *8vo, pp.* 119. New York, 1849

346 New York. Almanacks. The *American* Almanack. For the Years of Christian Account, 1731, 1732, and 1733. Printed by *Titan Leeds*, Philomat, 3 *vols.*, 12*mo.* Printed and sold by *William Bradford* in *New York*, and *Andrew Bradford*, *Philadelphia.*

1731, 1732, 1733

347 New York. Almanacks. The American Almanack. For the Years of *Christian* Account, 1737, 1738, 1739, 1742, and 1743. By Titan Leeds. 5 *vols.*, 12*mo,* *New York*: Printed and sold by *William Bradford,* 1737, 1738, 1739, 1742, and 1743

Excessively rare.

The Almanac for the year 1739 *has a special historical interest on account of its authenticating the date of William Bradford's birth, in regard to which there has been so much controversy, See Calendar for the month of May;* "The Printer Born the 20th, 1663." *Wallace, in his* "*Commemorate Address at the Celebration of the* 200*th Birth-day of Bradford,*" *refers to the Almanac of this year* (1739). *See pages* 19, 20, *and* 102.

348 New York. Almanacks. The American Almanack. For the Year of *Christian Account,* 1741. By Titan Leeds, *Philomat.*

Philadelphia: *Printed and Sold by* Andrew Bradford, 1741

349 New York. Poor Will's Almanac, for the Years of *Christian Account,* 1744 and 1750. By William Birkett. 2 *vols.*

Philadelphia: *Printed and Sold by* William Bradford, 1744; I. Warner and C. Bradford, 1750.

350 New York. American Country Almanac for the

Years of Christian Account, 1747, 1748, 1751, 1752, and 1754. By THOMAS MORE, *Philodespot.* 5 *vols.*

New York: *Printed and Sold by* J. Parker, 1747, 1748, 1751, 1752, 1754

351 NEW YORK. ASTRONOMICAL DIARY, or an ALMANACK for the Year of our LORD CHRIST, 1753. By ROGER SHERMAN.

New York: Printed and sold by *Henry De Forest*, 1753.

In all 9 *vols.*, 12*mo.* New York, and Philadelphia, 1741–44–47–48–50–51–52–53–54.

Scarce.

352 NEW YORK. "A MAP of the Country of THE FIVE NATIONS, belonging to the Province of NEW YORK, and of the LAKES, near which the Nations of FAR INDIANS Live, with part of CANADA and River St. Lawrence." *Small folio, in passepartout.* 37 00

New York: Printed and Published by William Bradford, 1727.

In fine condition, and of excessive rarity.

This Map was published by BRADFORD *to accompany the original edition of* COLDEN'S FIVE INDIAN NATIONS, *and was the* FIRST *one issued in the* COLONY OF NEW YORK.

353 NEW YORK. Anthology of New Netherland; or, Translations from the Early Dutch Poets of New York; with Memoirs of their Lives, by Henry C. Murphy. *Portrait of Steendam, fac-similes, etc. Royal* 8*vo, uncut.* 7 00

75 COPIES PRIVATELY PRINTED. New York, 1865

Bradford Club Series, No. 4.
Morrell, $13.00.

354 NEW YORK. [De Forest, T. R.] Olden Time in New York, by Those Who Knew. 12*mo, half crimson levant morocco, gilt top, uncut.* 2 25

New York, 1833

Morrell, unbound, $1.75.

355 De Peyster, Frederic. Early Political History of New York. Address delivered before the New York Historical Society, on its Sixtieth Anniversary, Tuesday, November 22, 1864. *Beautiful Portrait of Luther Bradish, engraved by Burt. Royal* 8vo., *uncut.*
Large Paper ; *but few printed.* New York, 1865

356 New York. Francis, John W. Old New York ; or, Reminiscences of the Past Sixty Years. With a Memoir of the Author, by Henry T. Tuckerman. *Portraits on India Paper, etc.* Unique Copy, *being extended to* Two *Volumes. With extra Title Pages, and* Illustrated *by the insertion of* 158 Plates, *consisting of Portraits, Views, etc., and including some of the rarest engravings, illustrative of New York, ever gathered together. There is also inserted an original autograph note (New York, Aug.* 10, 1806) *of* Hugh Gaine, *the Printer.* 2 *vols.*, 8*vo, full rich green levant morocco, gilt back, gilt top, uncut.*
Large Paper ; 100 *copies printed.* New York, 1865

In collecting the Illustrations for these volumes, the RARITY *and* CONDITION *of the plates has been more of a* DESIDERATUM *than to gather together a large number, the prevalent mania for* OVERFLOWING *a work with pictures giving it more the appearance of a* SCRAP BOOK. *To those engaged in illustrating "Dr. Francis's* Old New York," *the accompanying list of some of the* RARER *portraits, etc., inserted in the above volumes, may not be uninteresting.*

Mrs. Alsop, Luther Bradish, George Bancroft, William Bartram, Samuel Bard, John Bard, Matthew Carey, Henry Cruger, William Cobbett, J. S. Copley, Captain Jonathan Carver, George Frederick Cooke, William Dunlap, A. B. Durand, Lorenzo Dow, Citizen Genet, Elias Hicks, Philip Hone, Dr. Hosack, Washington Irving, Incledon, John Jay, Fanny Kemble, Edmund Kean, Madame Malibran, Dr. John M. Mason, Dr. Mitchell, Dr. Miller, Dr. Mott, Governeur Morris, Macready, Dr. Ogilvie, John Pintard, Elihu Palmer, Hiram Powers, Priestley, Tom Paine, C. W. Peale, James K. Paulding, Capt. Riley, Dr. Stiles, Dr. Sprague, Elihu H. Smith, R. C. Sands, Peter Stuyvesant, Alexander Wilson, Dr. Waterhouse, Sir Peter Warren Hugh Williamson, etc., etc.

Also Views of the Elgin Botanic Gardens, Columbia College, etc., etc.

357 New York. Francis, John W. New York During the

Last Half Century: A Discourse in Commemoration of the *Fifty-third Anniversary* of the New York Historical Society, and of the Dedication of their New Edifice (November 17, 1857). 8*vo*, *uncut*.

New York, 1857

Original edition of Dr. Francis's "Old New York;" scarce, in uncut condition.

358 New York. Ireland, Joseph N. Records of the New York Stage, from 1750 to 1860. *Vignette Portraits. Extended to Four Volumes, and Illustrated by the insertion of* 50 *Plates, consisting of Portraits of Fanny Kemble, Ellen Tree, Clara Fisher, Mrs. Wood, Miss Phillips, Cooke, Kean, Forrest, Macready, Edwin Booth, Dowton, Braham, Incledon, Hamblin, Sheridan Knowles, Major Noah, Harwood, Wallack, etc., etc., with autograph Letters of Charlotte Cushman, Burton, and others.* 2 *vols.*, *extended to* 4, *with extra title pages*, 8*vo*, *half morocco*, *gilt top*, *uncut*.

New York: T. H. Morrell, 1866-67

Only 200 Copies Printed.
"*The acknowledged standard work on the Drama in America.*"

359 New York. Journal of a Voyage to New York, and a *Tour in several of the American Colonies* in 1676-80, by Jasper Dankers and Peter Sluyter, of Wiewerd, in Friesland. Translated from the Original Manuscript in Dutch, and Edited by Henry C. Murphy. *Plates. Royal* 8*vo*., *pp*. 440, *uncut*.

Brooklyn, 1867

Large Paper; 100 *copies printed; scarce.*
Forms Vol. 1 *of the Long Island Historical Society Publications.*

360 New York. New York City During the Revolution: A Collection of Original Papers, Published from the

Original MSS. in the Possession of the Mercantile Library Association. *Map, 4to, cloth, uncut.*

New York, 1861

Privately Printed for the Association.

Morrell, morocco, extra plates, etc., $140 ; Fowle, $18 ; Allan, $9 ; Whitmore, $7 ; Bruce, half Russia, $7.

361 NEW YORK. Proceedings of TAMMANY SOCIETY, or Columbia Order, on LAYING THE CORNER-STONE of their New Hall on Fourteenth Street, and Celebrating the Ninety-first Anniversary of the Declaration of Independence, at Irving Hall, Thursday, July 4th, 1867. Also, a BRIEF HISTORY of the ORIGIN and EARLIER HISTORY of the Society. Published by order of the Tammany Society. *Views of Old and New Tammany Hall.* 28 *Plates inserted, including portraits, some very rare, of James Madison, Marinus Willett, John Pintard, Philip Freneau, Stephen Allen, Walter Bowne, Ogden Hoffman, Gulian C. Verplanck, Dewitt Clinton, etc. Also a number of scarce local views. 8vo, half green morocco, gilt top.* New York, 1867

362 NEW YORK. SMITH, WILLIAM. History of the Province of New York, from the First Discovery to the Year MDCCXXXII. To which is annexed, a Description of the Country, with a short Account of the Inhabitants, their Trade, Religion, and Political State, etc. *Rare "View of Fort George, with the City of New York," inserted. 4to, full levant morocco, gilt, by Matthews.* London, 1757

Fine copy, Very scarce.
Contains the plate of Oswego, often wanting.
Wight, half calf, $33. Morrell, $24. Bruce, half morocco, $20.

363 NEW YORK. SMITH, WILLIAM. The History of the late Province of New York, from its Discovery to the Appointment of Governor Colden in 1762. *Portrait of*

Colden inserted. 2 *vols., 8vo, boards, uncut, rough edges.* New York, 1830

From the library of Commodore Charles Wilkes, with his autograph. Bruce, half morocco, $5.25 per vol. Whitmore, $4.25 per vol. H. A. Smith, $2.50 per vol.

364 NEW YORK. The CHARTER OF THE CITY OF NEW YORK; Printed by Order of the Mayor, Recorder, Alderman, and Commonalty of the City aforesaid. To which is Annexed, THE ACT OF THE GENERAL ASSEMBLY Confirming the same. *Folio, pp.* 52. *Full crimson levant morocco, rich gilt back, and inside borders, by Bedford.* New York: Printed by JOHN PETER ZENGER. 1735

Fine clean copy. Excessively rare.

NEW YORK. *See Denton, Daniel.* TRIAL OF ZENGER.

366 NEW JERSEY. A Bill in the Chancery of *New Jersey*, at the Suit of JOHN Earl of STAIR, and Others, Proprietors of the Eastern Division of *New Jersey*, against *Benjamin Bond*, and some other Persons of *Elizabeth Town*, distinguished by the name of the *Clinker Lot Right Men ;* with the PUBLICATIONS of the Council of the Proprietors of *East New Jersey*, etc., concerning the RIOTS committed in NEW JERSEY, and the Pretences of the Rioters and their Seducers. 3 *large Maps. Folio, pp.* 124, 39 *uncut. Of great rarity.*

PUBLISHED BY SUBSCRIPTION. Printed by *James Parker*, in *New York*, 1747 ; and a few copies are to be sold by him and *Benjamin Franklin* in *Philadelphia.*

NEW JERSEY. *See Smith, Samuel, History of New Jersey.*

368 NICHOLSON, JAMES B. Manual of the Art of Book-binding, etc., designed for the Practical Workman, the Amateur, and the Book Collector. *Plates and Specimens.* 12*mo, cloth.* Philadelphia, 1856

Roche, half mor., $2.50 : Morrell, $2.25.

369 Niles, H. Principles and Acts of the Revolution in America, or an Attempt to Collect and Preserve some of the Speeches, Orations and Proceedings, with Sketches and Remarks on Men and Things, and other fugitive and neglected pieces, belonging to the Revolutionary Period in the United States, etc. *Royal 8vo, half morocco, gilt top, uncut.* Baltimore, 1822

370 Norton, Charles B. Literary Letter, comprising American Papers of Interest, and a Catalogue of Rare and Valuable Books relative to America. *Plates and Facsimiles.* 6 *Nos.* *All published.* *Small 4to.* New York, 1857–60

These little pamphlets have become quite scarce, and contain, besides other valuable matter, the Bibliography of the State of Maine, prepared by the Hon. William Willis.

O'CALLAGHAN, E. B. List of the Editions of the Holy Scriptures and Parts Thereof, Printed in America previous to 1860; with Introduction and Biographical Notes. *Fac-similes of the Title Pages to Eliot's Indian Bible, etc.* *Royal 8vo, uncut.*
Only 150 Copies Printed. Albany, 1861

Fowle, $20; Wight, $9.50; Bruce, $6.25; Morrell, $6; Roche, $6.

372 Orations. British Cruelty, Oppression, and Murder. Oration Delivered by John Hancock, Esq., at Boston, in Commemoration of the *Boston Massacre*, March 5th, 1770; also an Oration Delivered by Dr. Joseph Warren, at Boston on the same Subject, etc., with an *Account of the Captivity of* Mrs. Jeremiah Howe, taken by the *Indians* at Hinsdale, N. H., July 27th, 1765. 12*mo, uncut.* *Rare.*

P. M. Davis, Publisher (no place), 1824

373 ORDERLY BOOK OF THE NORTHERN ARMY, at Ticonderoga and Mount Independence, from October 17th, 1776, to January 8th, 1777, with Biographical and Explanatory Notes, and an Appendix. *Portrait of General Gates, and Map, with inserted Portrait of Colonel Anthony Wayne. 4to, half morocco, gilt top, uncut.*

Albany, Munsell, 1859

LARGE PAPER; *only* 10 *copies printed.*
Munsell's Historical Series, No. 3.
Fowle, $27.50; Wight, $10.25.

374 THE SAME.
Small 4to, uncut.
LIMITED EDITION. Albany, Munsell, 1859

PAINE, THOMAS. The American Crisis, and a Letter to *Sir Guy Carleton,* on the Murder of CAPTAIN HUDDY, and the Intended Retaliation on CAPTAIN ASGILL, *of the Guards.* 8*vo, pp.* 293, *uncut, rough edges. Very rare.* London, 1788

376 PARKMAN, JR., FRANCIS. History of the Conspiracy of Pontiac, and the War of the North American Tribes against the English Colonies after the Conquest of Canada. *Maps, Plate, "Pontiac's Fire Raft" inserted. Thick Royal* 8*vo, cloth, uncut.*
LARGE PAPER; 75 *Copies printed.* Boston, 1866

Morrell $7.00.

377 PARKMAN, JR., FRANCIS. France and England in North America. A Series of Historical Narratives. Pioneers of France in the New World. *Fine Portrait on India paper, and Map. Royal* 8*vo, cloth, uncut.*
LARGE PAPER; 75 *copies printed.* Boston, 1866

Morrell, $7.

378 Parkman, Jr., Francis. France and England in North America. A Series of Historical Narratives. The Jesuits in North America in the Seventeenth Century. *Map. Thick Royal* 8*vo, cloth, uncut.*
Large Paper ; 75 *copies printed.* Boston, 1867

379 Pattie, James O. Personal Narrative of, of Kentucky, during an Expedition from St. Louis to the Pacific Ocean, in which he and his Father, who accompanied him, Suffered unheard-of Hardships and Dangers, had various Conflicts with the Indians, and were made Captives, in which Captivity his Father Died. With a Description of the Country, etc. Edited by Timothy Flint. 8*vo, sheep ; scarce.*
Cincinnatti, 1833

Wight, $5.00 ; Fisher, $4.00 ; H. A. Smith, $3.50.

380 Paulding, James K. The Diverting History of John Bull and Brother Jonathan. By Hector Bull-us. Third Edition, improved. 4 *plates,* "*Jonathan throwing the Tea-Kettle at Bull's Head,*" *etc.* 12*mo, pp.* 114, *bds., uncut, rough edges. Rare.* Philadelphia, 1827

381 Paulding. Report of the Select Committee on Erecting a Monument to the Memory of *John Paulding,* with an Address to the Mayor of the City of New York. 12 *plates inserted ; portraits of Arnold, Paulding, etc.* 8*vo, half green levant morocco, gilt back and edges, by Matthews.*
Only 500 Copies Printed. New York, 1827

382 Peabody. Account of the Proceedings at the Dinner given by Mr. George Peabody to the Americans connected with the Great Exhibition, etc., on the 27th October, 1851. *Royal* 8*vo, cloth, gilt.*
London : Pickering, 1851

Large Paper. *Printed for private distribution.*

383 PEALE, REMBRANDT. Notes on Italy. Written during a Tour in the years 1829 and 1830. *Autograph Letter inserted.* 8*vo*, *boards*, *uncut*, *rough edges.*
Philadelphia, 1831

384 PEMAQUID PAPERS. Papers Relating to PEMAQUID and Parts adjacent, in the Present State of Maine, known *as Cornwall County*, when under the *Colony of New York.* Compiled from Official Records, etc., by Franklin B. Hough. 8*vo*, *uncut.*
LIMITED EDITION. Albany, 1856

Fowle, thick paper, half morocco, $16.

385 PENN. Original Autograph Letters, etc., of

ADMIRAL PENN.	Document signed, 1 p., folio,	1666
WILLIAM PENN.	Autograph Letter signed, 4 pp., 4to,	1686
HANNAH PENN.	" " " 2pp., "	1717
JOHN PENN.	" " " 2pp., "	1787
JULIANA PENN *to Henry Laurens*	" 2pp., "	1782

Portraits of William Penn, Admiral Penn, etc. Beautifully inlaid, 4*to size, and bound in full brown levant morocco, gilt edges.*
Collected and arranged, New York, 1868

386 PENNSYLVANIA. A Brief View of the Conduct of Pennsylvania for the Year 1755; so far as it affected the General Service of the *British Colonies*, particularly the Expedition under the late GENERAL BRADDOCK. With an Account of the Shocking Inhumanities committed by Incursions of the *Indians* upon the Province in *October* and *November*, etc. Interspersed with several interesting Anecdotes and original Papers, relating to the *Politics* and *Principles* of the People called QUAKERS; being a Sequel to a late well known Pamphlet, intitled A Brief State of Pennsylvania, etc. *Portrait of Braddock, and rare Engraving of "Braddock's Defeat," inserted.* 8*vo*, *pp.* 88, *half morocco, gilt top, by Bradstreet. Scarce.* London, 1756

387 Pennsylvania Hospital. Some *Account* of the *Pennsylvania Hospital*, from its First *Rise* to the beginning of the *Fifth Month*, called *May*, 1754. With the *Continuation*, from the First of *May*, 1754, to the Fifth of *May*, 1761. With a List of the *Contributors*, of the *Legacies* bequeathed, etc. *Both parts complete. View of the Hospital inserted. Small 4to, pp.* 77, *half brown morocco ; very rare.*

Philadelphia : Printed by B. Franklin and D. Hall.

1754-1761

Fine copy ; both parts seldom met with, the two title pages having Franklin and Hall's Imprint.

Wight, calf, without the Continuation, $21 ; Whitmore, without the Continuation, $10.

388 [Peters.] General History of Connecticut, from its First Settlement under George Fenwick, Esq., to its Latest Period of Amity with Great Britain, including a *Description of the Country*, and many curious and interesting Anecdotes. With an Appendix, wherein new and true Sources of the present Rebellion in America are pointed out ; together with the particular Part taken by the People of Connecticut in its Promotion. By a Gentleman of the Province. *8vo, pp.* 436, *full crimson crushed levant morocco, rich gilt back, inside borders and edges, by Bedford. Excessively rare.*

London : Printed for the Author, 1781

Splendid copy, perfectly spotless, and with large margins, having the appearance of a LARGE PAPER *copy.*

Contains a wonderful account of the upper Cohoes Falls, " where water is consolidated, without frost, by pressure, by swiftness, between the pinching sturdy rocks, to such a degree of induration, that no iron crow can be forced into it." Also a curious account of the ancient custom of courtship by " bundling."

" The anthor was Dr. Samuel A. Peters, a refugee. He resided in England from 1774 to 1805, when he returned to America, and died in New York in 1826, at the age of 90."

Bruce, half calf, $19.

389 PHELPS, RICHARD H. History of Newgate, of Connecticut, at Simsbury, now East Granby; its insurrections and Massacres, the Imprisonment of the Tories in the Revolution, and the Working of its Mines. Also, some account of the State Prison at Wethersfield. *Portrait and woodcut. Small 4to, uncut.*

Munsell, Albany, 1860

LARGE PAPER: *Very few copies printed.*
Fowle, $9.

390 PICKET, ALBERT JAMES. History of Alabama, and incidentally of Georgia and Mississippi, from the earliest period. Third edition. *Plates.* 2 *vols.*, 12*mo, half calf.* Charleston, 1851

Best edition, very scarce.
Morrell, $5.75 per vol. H. A. Smith, $4 per vol.

391 POPE, ALEXANDER. Essay on Man, Enlarged and Improved by the Author. With notes Critical and Explanatory. *Small 8vo, pp.* 46. *Scarce.*

New York: Printed by HUGH GAINE, at the Bible, in Hanover Square, 1786

392 POTTER, ISRAEL R. Life and Remarkable Adventures of, (a Native of Cranston, Rhode Island), who was a Soldier in the AMERICAN REVOLUTION, and took a distinguished part in the *Battle of Bunker Hill, etc., etc. Curious Woodcut Portrait of Potter, crying "Old Chairs to Mend."* 12*mo, half calf. Scarce.*

Providence, 1824

Morrell, $7.25. Fisher, $5.

393 POUCHOT. MEMOIR UPON THE LATE WAR IN NORTH AMERICA, between the French and English, 1755–'60; followed by Observations upon the Theatre of Actual War, and by New Details concerning the Manners and Customs of the Indians; with Topographical Maps. Translated and edited by Franklin B. Hough, with

additional Notes and Illustrations. *Maps and Plates: with extremely rare contemporary print of the "Taking of Quebeck" inserted.* 2 *vols.*, 4*to, half crimson crushed levant morocco, gilt top, uncut, by Matthews.*
Roxbury, Mass., 1866

LARGE PAPER: *only* 50 *copies.*

394 PRESIDENTS OF THE UNITED STATES. ORIGINAL AUTOGRAPH LETTERS OF THE PRESIDENTS OF THE UNITED STATES. Consisting of full letters entirely in the autograph, and signed by every President, from GEORGE WASHINGTON to ANDREW JOHNSON, inclusive, making in all 17 letters.

GEORGE WASHINGTON. *The great historical interest attached to the letter of Washington, written on the occasion of the burning of the village of Kingston, New York, by the British, in* 1772, *will warrant its being printed entire.*

GENTLEMEN:—I receive with peculiar pleasure the affectionate address of the Trustees of the Freeholders and Commonalty of the Town of Kingston,—your polite and friendly reception of me is a proof of its sincerity.

While I view with indignation the marks of a wanton and cruel enemy, I perceive with the highest satisfaction that the heavy calamity which befel this flourishing Settlement seems but to have added to the Patriotic spirit of its Inhabitants; and that a new town is fast rising out of the ashes of the old.

That you and your worthy Constituents may long enjoy the Freedom for which you have so nobly contended is the sincere wish of

Gentn. Yr. most obedt. & Hble. Sevt.

GEO. WASHINGTON.

Kingston, N. Y., 16th Nov., 1782.

JOHN ADAMS, Quincy, July, 1802.

Interesting letter relative to the Yellow Fever in Philadelphia.

THOMAS JEFFERSON, Monticello, October, 20th, 1815.

JAMES MADISON, Montpelier, January 20th, 1834.

JAMES MONROE, Philadelphia, February 28th, 1791.

JOHN QUINCY ADAMS, Boston, March 27th, 1794.

ANDREW JACKSON, Senate Chamber, (Washington,) May 22nd, 1824.

MARTIN VAN BUREN, Lindenwold, March 9th, 1856.

WILLIAM HENRY HARRISON, Cincinnati, October 27th, 1840.

JOHN TYLER, Sherwood Forest, Charles City County, Va., November 16, 1848.

JAMES K. POLK, Washington City, December 10th, 1827.

ZACHARY TAYLOR, Baton Rouge, Louisiana, June 20th, 1848.

MILLARD FILLMORE, Buffalo, N. Y., August 22d, 1856.

FRANKLIN PIERCE, to *Hon. J. Davis, Secretary of War*, no date.

JAMES BUCHANAN, Wheatlands near Lancaster, Penn, August 29th, 1856.

ABRAHAM LINCOLN, Executive Mansion, March 7, 1861.

ANDREW JOHNSON, Greenville, Tenn., May, 1859.

Fine Portraits accompany each letter.

These letters, all ONE PAGE in length, have been beautifully inlaid, in heavy white paper, quarto size.

This unique volume is superbly bound by MATTHEWS in full green levant morocco, full gilt back and sides, elegantly hand-tooled, with rich inside borders and linings of green moire antique. The binding of this volume could not be duplicated for $75.

Extract from "The Nation," November 28, 1867.

"Speaking of autographs, we find in Mr. Morrell's collection many of Revolutionary heroes and many of artists, etc. He has, in a dress almost extravagantly fine, *autograph letters* of all the PRESIDENTS FROM WASHINGTON DOWN TO MR. JOHNSON. The letters are none of them long; each is written on one page of writing paper, and it was therefore possible to make them an inlaid volume. Mr. Lincoln's is short and, characteristically, is expressive of that friendliness and kindness which constituted not the smallest of his claims to the admiration of his countrymen and all mankind. It reads as follows: 'Whom it may concern. William Johnson, a colored boy, and bearer of this, has been with me about twelve months; and has been, so far, as I believe, honest, faithful, sober, industrious, and handy as a servant. A. Lincoln.' The book contains portraits engraved on steel of each of the Presidents, and is a curiosity which it would not be easy to duplicate."

395 PRINCE, THOMAS. CHRONOLOGICAL HISTORY OF NEW-ENGLAND, in the form of Annals; being A summary and exact Account of the most material *Transactions* and *Occurrences* relating to THIS COUNTRY, in the Order of Time wherein they happened from the *Discovery* by CAPT. GOSNOLD, in 1602, to the arrival of Governor BELCHER in 1730, with An Introduction, &c. *Portrait inserted.* (*Vol.* 1.) *Part I and part II. Small* 8*vo, full green levant morocco, gilt back and edges, by Matthews.*
Boston, N. E. *Printed by Kneeland and Green, for S. Gerrish,* 1736

VERY SCARCE.
Morrell, $25. Roche, $23.

396 PRINCE, THOMAS. Sermon at the *South Church* in *Boston,* N. E. On the GENERAL THANKSGIVING, Thursday, *July* 18, 1745. Occasion'd by Taking the City of *Louisbourg,* on the Isle of *Cape-Breton,* by *New-England* Soldiers, assisted by a *British* Squadron. 8*vo, pp.* 32.
BOSTON, Printed: LONDON, Reprinted, 1746

397 PRINCE, THOMAS. Sermon at the *South Church* in *Boston,* Nov. 27, 1746, Being the Day of the ANNIVERSARY THANKSGIVING in the *Province* of the *Massachusetts Bay* in NEW-ENGLAND, etc. 8*vo, pp.* 36.
BOSTON, Printed: LONDON, Reprinted, 1747

398 PROCLAMATIONS FOR THANKSGIVING, issued by the Continental Congress, President Washington, by the National and State Governments on the Peace of 1815, and by the Governors of New York, &c., &c., with An Introduction and Notes (by F. B. Hough.) *Royal,* 8*vo, uncut.*
Albany, 1858

PRIVATELY PRINTED: *Only* 150 *copies.*
A few portraits inserted.

399 PROUD, ROBERT. The History of Pennsylvania, in North America, from the Original Institution and Settlement of that Province, under the first *Proprietor* and *Governor*, WILLIAM PENN, in 1681, till after the year 1742. With an Introduction, Appendix, etc. *Portrait of William Penn, and Map.* 2 *vols.*, 8*vo*, *boards uncut, rough edges.* Philadelphia, 1797

FINE CLEAN COPY: *Excessively rare in the original uncut condition.*

Fisher, half morocco, uncut, $11.50 per vol. H. A. Smith, half morocco, uncut, $11.50 per vol. Wight, half morocco, uncut, $11 per vol. Bruce, $6.63 per vol. Morrell, $6.25 per vol. Roche, $6 per vol.

400 PSALMS. The Whole Book of Psalmes, faithfully Translated into English Metre, whereunto is prefixed a Discourse declaring not only the Lawfullness, but also the Necessity of the Heavenly Ordinance of Singing Scripture Psalmes in the Churches of God. Imprinted 1640. A *literal* reprint of the BAY PSALM-BOOK; being the earliest New-England version of the Psalms, and the *first book* printed in America. 8*vo*, *full purple levant morocco, gilt edges, back and sides, inside linings of green crushed levant with rich and elaborate toolings, by Pawson & Nicholson.*

Charles B. Richardson, New York, 1862

PRIVATELY PRINTED; *and only* 50 *copies. Three were destroyed by fire at the Irving buildings. Exceedingly scarce.*

Binding cost $30.

Fowle, $60. Whitmore, thick paper, $50. Morrell, $37.50. Bruce, thick paper, $37. Roche, $31. Wight, $20.

401 PUTNAM. Memoirs of the Life, Adventures and Military Exploits of Israel Putnam, Senior Major-General in the Revolutionary Army of the United States, and next in Rank to General Washington. 12*mo*, *boards.* Ithaca, 1839

402 [PUTNAM, GEORGE P.] Pocket Memorandum Book during a Ten Weeks' Trip to Italy and Germany in 1847.

Printed on blue letter paper. Small 4to., 144 *pp., cloth.* New York, 1848

PRIVATELY PRINTED. *Only* 20 *copies. Very scarce.*
"These brief notes from a pocket memorandum book and 'written on the wing,' have been printed in the LITERARY WORLD, *and a very few copies are struck off in this form, chiefly for private friends."*

QUINCY, Jr., JOSIAH. Observations on the act of Parliament commonly called the BOSTON PORT BILL; with Thoughts on Civil Society and Standing Armies. *8vo, pp.* 60. Philadelphia, 1774

A few leaves slightly spotted.

RAMSAY, DAVID. The History of the Revolution of South Carolina, from a British Province to an Independent State. *Maps. Portrait of Ramsay inserted.* 2 *vols., 8vo, calf. Fine clean copy. Rare.* Trenton, 1785

Morrell, uncut, $15 per vol. Roche, uncut, $8,25 per vol.

405 RAMSAY, DAVID. The History of the American Revolution. New Edition. 2 *vols., 8vo, uncut, rough edges.* London, Stockdale, 1793

Fine clean copy.

406 RANDOLPH, JOHN. Letters to a young Relative; embracing a Series of Years, from early Youth, to Mature Manhood. *Portrait inserted. 8vo, boards, uncut, rough edges.* Philadelphia, 1834

Very scarce in uncut condition.

407 READ, Jr., JOHN MEREDITH. Historical Inquiry concerning Henry Hudson, his Friends, Relatives, and Early Life, his connection with the Muscovy company and Discovery of Delaware Bay. *Arms of Henry Hudson in Gold and colors.* 2 *Fine engravings inserted, "Land-*

ing of Henry Hudson," *and "Hudson's Interview with the Indians."* *4to, half green morocco, gilt top, uncut.* Albany, 1866

LARGE PAPER: *Only* 50 *copies printed.*
Roche, $11. Morrell, $11.

408 REBELLION. BARKER, JACOB. The Rebellion; Its consequences, and the Congressional Committee, denominated the Reconstruction Committee with their action. By Investigator. *Portrait of Jacob Barker inserted.* *8vo, pp.* 248, *half bound. Scarce.* New Orleans, 1866

409 REBELLION. Draft Riots. The Bloody Week! Riot, Murder and Arson; containing a Full Account of this Wholesale Outrage on Life and Property, Accurately prepared from Official Sources, by Eye Witnesses, etc. *8vo, pp.* 32. *Rare.* New York, 1863

410 REBELLION. Envelopes. A collection of over 600 UNION AND REBEL ENVELOPES, all different, consisting of Portraits, Flags, Shields, State Arms, Soldiers and Sailors, Cannons, Eagles, Comic Mottoes, etc., etc., issued during the late Rebellion. *Neatly mounted in Scrap Books.* 2 *vols. 4to, half morocco.* New York, and other places.

411 REBELLION. Government Sale. Catalogue of an immense Collection of Library Books, etc., to be sold at Auction By Order and under the Direction of HIRAM BARNEY, Esq., Collector of the Port of N. Y., on Monday evening, Nov. 17th, 1862, etc. By Bangs, Merwin & Co. *8vo. Scarce.* New York, 1862

Sale countermanded, and catalogue suppressed.

412 REBELLION. Historical Reminiscences. Scrap Book containing a collection of Rebel and Union Newspapers, Hand Bills, Placards, Confederate Bonds, Money,

Badges, Passes, Oaths of Allegiance, Songs, Union Calico, Bogus Extras, etc., etc., neatly mounted in folio Scrap Book.

Among the rare curiosities in this volume, is an original copy of the "Daily Citizen, Vicksburg, Miss., July 2, 1863," printed on *wall paper* with *Postscript* announcing the SURRENDER TO GEN. GRANT. Extras with account of "Attack on Fort Sumter," "North Carolina Times," printed on *Straw Paper*, Original Placard issued by the War Department, April 20, 1865, offering "$100,000 REWARD FOR THE MURDERER OF OUR LATE BELOVED PRESIDENT," "Draft Riot" Handbill, New York, July 14, 1863, calling a Meeting of the Merchants, Bankers, etc., for Organization and Enrollment "*to take immediate Action in the present crisis. Military now engaged with the Mob. The Mayor's House being Sacked and Torn Down!!*" Excessively rare Placard, issued in New York, June 30, 1863, calling upon GENERAL HALLECK to *send troops to support the Union Army*, to "CONQUER LEE, OR RESIGN."

413 REBELLION. JAMISON, D. F. Life and Times of Bertrand Du Guesclin: a History of the Fourteenth Century. *Portrait.* 2 *vols.*, 8*vo*, *cloth*, *uncut.* London, 1864

Beautifully printed, with initial letters, and head and tail pieces.
"*The Author was President of the Convention in Charleston, S. C., which passed the ordinance of Secession. It was printed in London, and a number of copies were taken in a blockade runner.*
Roche, $5 per vol.

414 REBELLION. Life of Thomas J. Jackson. (STONEWALL JACKSON.) By an ex-Cadet. Second Edition, Revised and Enlarged by the author. 12*mo*, *pp.* 196. Richmond, 1864

415 REBELLION. McCLELLAN. Eight Pamphlets on General McClellan's Campaign, when Commander of the Army of the Potomac, 1861–62. 8 Pamphlets. 8*vo and* 12*mo*. *Some scarce.* v. p. v. y.

416 REBELLION. Pamphlets. A collection of Fifty Pamphlets relative to the late Rebellion in America, by Lossing, Curtis, Thayer, Ingersoll, Moore, Gen. Meagher, Stillè, Laboulaye, etc., etc. *Some very rare, having been suppressed.* 50 *Pamphlets*, 8*vo*, 12*mo*, *etc.*

417 REBELLION. Report of Lieut. General U. S. Grant, of the Armies of the United States. 1864–'65. *Portraits of Gens. Grant, Sherman and Burnside inserted.* 8*vo, half morocco, gilt top.* Washington, 1865

Presentation Copy, with autograph, "U. S. Grant, Lt. Gen." Autographs of the PRESIDENT ELECT *are very rare.*

418 REBELLION. Tucker, Judge Beverly. The Partisan Leader; a Novel, and an Apocalypse of the Origin and Struggles of the Southern Confederacy. Originally published in 1836. Now Re-published and edited by Rev. Thomas A. Ware. 8*vo, pp.* 220. Richmond, 1862

419 REBELLION. Uniform and Dress of the ARMY of the CONFEDERATE STATES. *Plates. Inserted in this rare volume is a beautiful proof portrait of* GEN. ROBERT E. LEE, *in uniform, with his autograph attached to check on Bank of Commerce, New York,* 31 *May,* 1841, "*R. E. Lee, Capt. Engnrs. on ac. Fort Hamilton.*" *Also Portrait and Autograph Letter of* JEFFERSON DAVIS, 1 *p.,* 4*to.* (*Concordia,* 16*th November,* 1848.) *Royal* 4*to, boards.* Richmond, 1861

Excessively rare.

420 RECORD OF THE COURT OF UPLAND, *in Pennsylvania,* 1676 to 1681. And a Military Journal kept by Major E. Denny, 1781 to 1795. *Portraits of Major Denny and Gen. Harmar, etc.* 8*vo, cloth.* Philadelphia, 1860

421 RECUEIL D'ESTAMPES REPRESENTANT les Diffèrents Evenemens de la Guerre qui a procure l'Indépendence aux Etats Unis de l'Amérique, *A series of sixteen beautiful steel Engravings, by Godfrey, and M. Ponce, illustrative of the principal events of the Revolutionary*

War, with descriptions (also engraved). Oblong, 4*to*, *calf, gilt.*

BEAUTIFUL IMPRESSIONS. Paris, [1790.]

Contains views of the Battles of Lexington and Saratoga, Surrender of Lord Cornwallis, etc.

422 REED, WILLIAM B. Life and Correspondence of JOSEPH REED, Military Secretary of Washington, at Cambridge, Adjutant General of the Continental Army, etc. By his Grandson. *Portrait, with rare additional one inserted.* 2 *vols.*, 8*vo*, *cloth.*

Philadelphia, 1847

Wight, $4.50 per vol. H. A. Smith, sheets, $4.12 per vol. Morrell, sheets, $2.50 per vol.

423 REED AND CADWALADER. A Reprint of the Reed and Cadwalader Pamphlets. with an Appendix. *Royal* 8*vo*, *half morocco, gilt top, uncut.*

LIMITED EDITION PRINTED. [Philadelphia,] 1863

Fowle, $9. Wight, $3.50. Fisher, $3.

424 REES, JAMES. Dramatic Authors of America. *Portraits of William Dunlap, Edwin Forrest, and Mrs. Mowatt inserted.* 12*mo*, *half morocco, gilt top.*

Rare. Philadelphia, 1845

Morrell, extra plates, $5.25.

425 RHODE ISLAND. STATE OF AMERICAN REBEL PRISONERS EXCHANGED BY CARTEL, the 26th of November 1778, and the 25th of February, 1779. ORIGINAL MANUSCRIPT. 18 *pp. folio.*

426 RIEDESEL, MADAME DE. Letters and Memoirs relating to the War of American Independence, and the Capture of the German Troops at Saratoga. Translated from the Original German. 12*mo*, *boards, uncut, rough edges.*

Fine copy, scarce. New York, 1827

Inserted in this copy is the original " Embarkation Return of the Guards, of Men of British and German Regiments under the Conventions of Saratoga, etc.," signed by SIR GUY CARLETON, *June* 15, 1783. *Also Portraits of Gen. Riedesel, Lady Ackland, Engraving of Burgoyne's Surrender, etc.*

Fisher, autographs, etc., $21.50. Morrell, extra plates, etc., $14. Wight, $10.25. Whitmore, $8. Roche, $8.

427 ROBIN, ABBE. New Travels through North America. In a Series of Letters; Exhibiting the History of the Victorious Campaign of the Allied Armies, under His Excellency, Gen. Washington, and the Count De Rochambeau, in the year 1781, etc. Also, Narrations of the Capture of General Burgoyne and Lord Cornwallis, with their Armies; etc., etc. Translated from the Original of the Abbé Robin; One of the Chaplains to the French Army in America. *Portrait of Count Rochambeau inserted. 8vo, full polished calf, gilt back, gilt top, uncut, by Bedford.*

Philadelphia, 1783

Splendid copy in the most perfect order of the excessively rare first edition, and almost impossible to duplicate in uncut condition.

428 ROBINSON, CONWAY. An Account of Discoveries in the West until 1519, and of VOYAGES to and along the *Atlantic Coast of North America, from* 1520 *to* 1573. Prepared for the "Virginia Historical and Philosophical Society." *8vo, pp.* 491, *cloth.* Richmond, 1848

Whitmore, 4.50. Wight, $4. H. A. Smith, half calf, $2.50.

429 ROGERS, MAJOR ROBERT. Journals: containing an Account of the several excursions he made under the Generals who commanded upon the Continent of NORTH AMERICA, during the late War, etc.

CONCISE ACCOUNT OF NORTH AMERICA: containing a description of the several BRITISH COLONIES, on that Continent, etc., with an Account of the several Nations and Tribes of *Indians*, etc., their Customs, Manners, Government, Numbers, etc., etc.

2 vols. 8vo, green levant morocco, gilt inside borders. *Beautiful copies. Rare.*

London: Printed for the AUTHOR, 1765

"Major Rogers headed, with much reputation, the provincial troops called Rangers, during the whole course of what were called the *French* wars in America. To this brave, active, judicious officer, it is that the public are indebted for the most satisfactory account yet published of the interior parts of America."—*Monthly Review.*

430 ROWLANDSON, MRS. MARY. Narrative of the Captivity and Removes of, who was taken by the *Indians* at the Destruction of Lancaster, in 1676. Written by Herself. 16mo, boards. Lancaster, 1828

Fisher, half morocco, $3.50. H. A. Smith, half morocco, $3.00.

431 RUSH, BENJAMIN. An Account of the Life and Character of CHRISTOPHER LUDWICK, late Citizen of Philadelphia, and Baker-General of the Army of the United States during the Revolutionary War. First published in the year 1801.
12*mo, boards.* Philadelphia, 1831

432 RUSSELL, WILLIAM. History of America, from its Discovery by Columbus to the Conclusion of the late War. With an APPENDIX, containing an Account of the RISE AND PROGRESS OF THE PRESENT UNHAPPY CONTEST BETWEEN GREAT BRITAIN AND HER COLONIES. *Numerous fine Plates, including Portraits of Columbus, Sir Walter Raleigh, Washington, Franklin, Sir Henry Clinton, etc., and the very rare View of "Fort George with the City of New York."* 2 *vols.,* 4*to., calf.*

London, 1778

The impressions of the many plates, are in this copy unusually fine.

SABINE, LORENZO. American Loyalists, or Biographical Sketches of Adherents to the British Crown in the War of Revolution. With a Preliminary Historical Essay. *Portrait of Gov. William Franklin inserted. Thick* 8*vo, cloth, uncut.* Boston, 1847.

434 Sabine, Lorenzo. Biographical Sketches of Loyalists of the American Revolution, with an Historical Essay. *Handsomely printed on toned paper.* 2 *vols.*, 8*vo, sheets folded.* Boston, 1864

Fowle, $5.00 per vol.

435 Sabine, Lorenzo. An Address before the *New England Historic-Genealogical Society*, Tuesday, September 13th, 1859. *The Two Hundredth Anniversary* of the Death of Major General James Wolfe, with Passages omitted in the delivery, and illustrative Notes and Documents. 31 *Plates inserted, including rare Portraits of Generals Wolfe, Amherst, Arnold, Lord Loudon, Barré, Pitt, and others, with View of Siege of Quebec, Death of Wolfe, etc.* 8*vo, half green morocco, gilt top, uncut.* Boston, 1859

436 Salem Witchcraft:—Comprising More Wonders of the Invisible World, Collected by *Robert Calef;* and Wonders of the Invisible World, by *Cotton Mather;* With Notes and Explanations by Sam'l P. Fowler. *Rubricated Title pages, portrait, etc.* 4*to, cloth, uncut.* Boston, 1865

Large Paper; few printed.
Morrell, $6.50. Roche, $3.00. Bruce, $3.00.

437 Sanderson, John. Biography of the Signers to the Declaration of Independence. 31 *portraits.* 9 *vols.* 8*vo boards, uncut, rough edges.* Philadelphia, 1820

Splendid copy, clean, with choice impressions of the portraits.
Wight, large paper, half Russia, uncut, $11.75 per vol. Fowle, $9.00 per vol. Morrell, $3.88 per vol. Whitmore, $3.00 per vol. H. A. Smith, $2.75 per vol. Bruce, $2.12 per vol.

438 Sargent, Winthrop. The History of an Expedition against Fort Du Quesne, in 1755, under Major-General Edward Braddock. Edited from the Original Manuscripts.

Plate and maps. 8*vo, cloth.*

Published by the Historical Society of Pennsylvania.

Philadelphia, 1855

Wight, half morocco, $4.25. Roche, $2.50. Whitmore, $2.25. H. A. Smith, $1.75.

439 SCHUYLKILL FISHING COMPANY. An Authentic Historical Memoir of the Schuylkill Fishing Company of the State in Schuylkill. From its Establishment on that Romantic Stream, near Philadelphia, in the year 1732, to the present time. By a Member. *Plate.*

8*vo, half levant morocco, gilt top, uncut ; scarce.*

Philadelphia, 1830

Fisher, cloth, $3.00. Wight, $2.63.

440 SCOTT, WINFIELD. Memoirs of Lieutenant-General Winfield Scott, LL. D. Written by himself. *Portraits. A number of plates inserted, including several rare portraits of Gen. Scott ; also his autograph, attached to check,* 1831. *Royal* 8*vo, cloth, uncut.*

New York, 1864

LARGE PAPER : *limited edition.*

441 SEDGWICK, THEODORE. Memoir of the Life of William Livingston, Member of Congress in 1774, 1775, and 1776, Delegate to the Federal Convention in 1787, and Governor of the State of New Jersey from 1766 to 1790, etc. *Portrait,* 8*vo, boards.* New York, 1833

Wight, $3.13. Morrell, $2.50. Whitmore, $1.75.

442 SEVENTY-SIX SOCIETY. The Publications of:

1. Papers in relation to the Case of SILAS DEANE. Now first published from the Original Manuscripts.
2. The Examination of JOSEPH GALLOWAY, ESQ., by a Committee of the House of Commons. Edited by Thomas Balch.
3. Papers relating to Public Events in MASSACHUSETTS preceding the American Revolution.

4. Papers relating chiefly to the MARYLAND Line during the Revolution. Edited by Thomas Balch.
4 *vols.* 8*vo*, *sheets folded.*
Philadelphia, 1855—57

LIMITED EDITIONS. *Excessively rare in this condition.*

Roche, half morocco, uncut, $6.00 per vol.

443 SHAKESPEARE. Tercentenary Celebration of the Birth of Shakespeare, by the New England Historic-Genealogical Society, at Boston, Mass., April 23d, 1864. *Fine proof portrait of Shakespeare inserted, also beautiful inlaid extra Title. Folio, half crimson morocco, gilt top, uncut.*
PRIVATELY PRINTED. Boston, 1864

LARGE PAPER; *only* 25 *copies printed.*

Morrell, extra plates, $14.00.

444 SIEGE OF QUEBEC. Memoirs of the Life and Gallant Exploits of the Old Highlander, Sergeant DONALD MACLEOD, who, having returned, wounded, with the Corpse of General Wolfe, from Quebec, was admitted an out-Pensioner of Chelsea Hospital, in 1759: and is now in the CIII'd year of his Age. *Fine Portrait of Serjeant Macleod.*
8*vo*, *half green morocco. Rare.*
London, 1791

445 SIEGE OF QUEBEC. Journal of the Principal Occurrences during the *Siege of Quebec* by the American Revolutionists under *Generals Montgomery and Arnold*, in 1775–76: Containing many Anecdotes of moment never yet published. Collected from some Old Manuscripts originally WRITTEN BY AN OFFICER, etc., with a *Preface* and *Illustrative Notes*, by W. T. P. SHORT.
Rare Portraits of Gens. Wolfe, Montgomery, and Arnold inserted, also proof engraving of the Death of

Montgomery. 8vo, pp. 111. *Green levant morocco, gilt. Scarce.* London, 1824

Bruce, half morocco, $7.00.

446 SIGNERS OF THE DECLARATION OF INDEPENDENCE. Book of the Signers: Containing Fac-Simile Letters of the Signers of the Declaration of Independence. With Sixty-one Engravings from Original Photographs and Drawings, of their Residences, Portraits, etc. UNIQUE AND VALUABLE COPY—having inserted TWENTY ORIGINAL AUTOGRAPH LETTERS AND DOCUMENTS SIGNED, OF FRANKLIN, JOHN ADAMS, HANCOCK, JEFFERSON, R. H. LEE, CHARLES CARROLL OF CARROLTON, ROBERT MORRIS, etc., etc.

Also 100 *Engravings, including Portraits of nearly all the Signers*—FRANKLIN, JEFFERSON, HANCOCK, ADAMS, CARROLL, etc., etc., *many being of the greatest beauty and rarity—and all inlaid, or mounted neatly on heavy plate paper.*

Views of the OLD STATE HOUSE, PHIL.—COATS OF ARMS OF THE DIFFERENT STATES—many being fine, choice proofs.

The *portraits* include a *full set* from Sanderson's Lives of the Signers—9 vols.

The letters and documents are as follows:

B. Franklin, A. L. S. 1756
Robert Morris, " 1793
Charles Carroll, " 1822
Jefferson, " 1813
R. H. Lee, " 1792
B. Rush, " 1803
E. Gerry, " 1780
S. Huntington, " 1795
Charles Thomson, " 1783
W. Paca, A. D. S. 1756
John Hancock, D. S. 1776

Phil. Livingston,	D. S.	1756
R. T. Paine,	"	1795
Geo. Clymer,	"	1809
" "	"	n. d.
James Wilson,	L. S.	1794
John Adams,	"	1819
John Witherspoon,	"	1775

John, Hart, Signature to Continental Bill, 1776

F. Hopkinson, Signature to Bill of Exchange, 1780

Extra Title page. Folio. Half green morocco, bevelled, gilt edges, gilt back.

LARGE PAPER: Only 99 copies.

Philadelphia, William Brotherhead, 1861

447 SIGNERS OF THE DECLARATION OF INDEPENDENCE. Book of the Signers: Containing Fac-Simile Letters of the Signers of the Declaration of Independence. Illustrated also with SIXTY-ONE ENGRAVINGS from Original Photographs and Drawings of their Residences, Portraits, etc.

Edited by William Brotherhead. *Beautiful Portrait on India paper of* THOMAS JEFFERSON *inserted. Folio, half purple levant morocco, gilt top, uncut.*

Philadelphia, 1861

LARGE PAPER: 99 *copies printed.*

Fowle, $30.

448 SILLIMAN, BENJAMIN. Remarks made on a Short Tour, between Hartford and Quebec, in the Autumn of 1819. *Engraved Title, Views of Lake George, Quebec, etc.* 12*mo, half morocco.* New Haven, 1820

449 SIMMS, J. R. Trappers of New York, or a Biography of *Nicolas Stoner* and *Nathaniel Foster;* together with Anecdotes of other celebrated Hunters, etc. *Plates.* 12*mo, cloth.* Albany, 1851

Fisher, half morocco, $2.00.

450 SIMMS, J. R. American Spy, or Freedom's Early Sacrifice; A Tale of the Revolution, Founded on Fact. *Frontispiece, Capt. Nathaniel Hale's Monument. Royal 8vo, uncut.* Munsell, Albany, 1857

LARGE PAPER: *only 28 copies.*
Fisher, half morocco, $4.00, Morrell, $2.75, Roche, hf mor., $2.75.

451 SIMMS, WILLIAM GILMORE. Army Correspondence of Colonel John Laurens in the years 1777–8. Now first printed from Original Letters addressed to his Father, HENRY LAURENS, President of Congress. With a Memoir by Wm. Gilmore Simms. *Fine Proof Portrait of Col. Laurens. Roy. 8vo, uncut.*
75 COPIES PRIVATELY PRINTED. New York, 1867
Bradford Club Series, No. 7.

This work was omitted under the head of LAURENS.

452 SIMMS, WILLIAM GILMORE. Life of Francis Marion. *Plates. Portrait and rare Autograph of Gen. Marion* (1781,) *inserted.* 12*mo, cloth.* New York, 1845

453 SMITH, CAPTAIN, JOHN. The GENERALL HISTORIE OF VIRGINIA, NEW-ENGLAND, AND THE SUMMER ISLES, with the names of the Adventurers, Planters, and *Governours* from their first beginning, anno 1584 to this present 1624. WITH THE PROCEEDINGS OF THESE SEVERALL COLONIES, *and the Accidents that befell them in all their Journyes and Discoveries.* Also the Maps and Descriptions of all those Countryes, their Commodities, People, Government, Customes, and Religion yet knowne. DIVIDED INTO SIX BOOKS. *By Captain* JOHN SMITH, *sometymes Governour in those Countryes and Admirall of* NEW-ENGLAND. *Engraved Title,* (*with Portraits and Coats of Arms*), *Map of* VIRGINIA, *Map of* NEW-ENGLAND, (*with Portrait of* CAPTAIN SMITH), *and Engraving of the* "FORTS."

Small folio, pp. 248, full polished sprinkled calf, gilt back and edges, and inside borders, by Pratt.

FIRST EDITION. LONDON. Printed by J. D. and I. H. for *Michael Sparkes.* 1624

Fine copy, clean, and with good margins. Excessively rare.

Unfortunately wants one Map.

454 SMITH, CAPTAIN JOHN. THE TRVE TRAVELS, ADVENTVRES AND OBSERVATIONS of *Captaine* IOHN SMITH, in *Europe, Asia, Affrica and America*, from *Anno Domini* 1593 to 1629. His Accidents and Sea Fights in the Straights; his Service and Stratagems of warre in *Hungaria, Transilvania, Wallachia* and *Moldavia*, against the *Turks*, and *Tartars;* his three single combats betwixt the *Christian* Armie and the *Turkes*, After how he was taken prisoner by the *Turks*, sold for a Slave, sent into *Tartaria*, etc.

Together with a Continuation of his Generall History of VIRGINIA, SUMMER ILES, NEW-ENGLAND, and their proceedings, since 1624, to this present 1629; as also of the new Plantations of the great River of the *Amazons*, the Iles of *St. Christopher, Mevis*, and *Barbados* in the *West Indies.* All written by actuall Authours, whose names you shall finde along the History.

Coat of Arms—on reverse of Title page. Small folio, pp. 60, *full polished calf, gilt back, edges and inside borders, by Bedford.*

LONDON, Printed by *F. H.* for *Thomas Slater*, and are to bee sold at the Blue Bible in *Greene Arbour.* 1630

Beautiful copy, with large margins. Excessively rare. Wants the Plate.

455 SMITH, CAPTAIN JOHN. The Trve Travels, Adventvres and Observations of Captaine Iohn Smith, in *Europe, Asia, Africke, and America;* beginning about the yeere

1593, and continued to this Present 1629. *Portrait and Engravings from the London edition of* 1629. 2 *vols.*, 8*vo.*, *boards, uncut, rough edges. Fine, clean copy. Scarce.* Richmond, 1819

Bruce, half morocco, uncut, $14.00 per vol. Morrell, $8.50 per vol. Whitmore, $7.00 per vol. H. A. Smith, $6.00 per vol. Roche. $5.25 per vol.

456 Smith, Capt. John. Advertisements for the Unexperienced Planters of New England, or Anywhere; or the Pathway to erect a Plantation. *Fac-simile of Smith's Map of New England* (1635). *Small* 4*to, cloth, uncut.* Boston, 1865

75 Copies Printed.

Fisher, $5.00. Morrell, $4.50.

457 Smith, Capt. John. Description of New England; Observations and Discoveries in the North of America in the year of our Lord 1614. With the Succefs of six Ships that went the next year, 1615. *Map. Small* 4*to, uncut.* Boston, 1865

75 Copies Printed.

Fisher, $5.00 Morrell, $4.50.

458 Smith, J. Spear. Memoir of the Baron De Kalb, read at the Meeting of the Maryland Historical Society, 7th January, 1858. 16 *Plates inserted, including beautiful drawing in pencil and sepia of De Kalb.* 8*vo, half green morocco, gilt top. Scarce.* Baltimore, 1858

Brought at Sale of my Library in 1866, $14, and re-purchased in 1867 at Sale of Mr. Elliott's Library.

459 Smith, Mrs. E. Oakes. Salamander; a Legend for Christmas, found amongst the papers of the late Ernst Helfenstein, edited by E. Oakes Smith. *Plates by Darley.* 8*vo, cloth gilt.* New York, 1848

The scene of this romantic story is laid among the hills and vales of the beautiful county of Rockland. In the introduction to this work, the editor refers to several incidents occurring in this region, relative to General Washington and the American Revolution.

460 SMITH, SAMUEL. THE HISTORY OF THE COLONY OF NOVA-CÆSARIA, or New-Jersey; containing an Account of its First Settlement Progrefsive Improvements, The Original and Present Constitution, and other Events, to the year 1721, with some particulars since; and A Short View of its Present State. *8vo, pp.* 574. *Full French bright gros grained crimson morocco, elegant, full gilt back, broad rich borders inside, and French filleted pannelled sides, edges gilt before sewed, by Bedford.* Burlington, N. J., 1765 5000

SPLENDID COPY.

With the exception of the unique UNCUT *copy in the possession of John A. Rice, Esq., of Chicago, this is probably the finest ever offered for sale.*

Roche, calf, $52. Whitmore, morocco, $35. Bruce, $27. Wight, calf, $26.50. H. A. Smith, half morocco, $25. Morrell, sheep, $21. Fisher, half sheep, $21.

461 SMITH, WILLIAM. History of the PROVINCE of NEW YORK, from the First Discovery to the Year MDCCXXXII. To which is annexed a Description of the Country, with a short Account of the Inhabitants, their Trade, Religious and Political State, and the Constitution of the Courts of Justice in that Colony. *Fine impression of the rare View of Oswego. 4to. Calf. Fine Copy.* London, 1757 1100

For quotation of prices, see NEW YORK. SMITH, WILLIAM.

462 SMITH, WILLIAM. Sermon Preached in *Christ-Church*, Philadelphia; Before the Provincial GRAND MASTER, and General Communication of *Free* and *Accepted* MASONS. On *Tuesday*, the 24th of *June*, 1755, being the *Grand Anniversary* of ST. JOHN, the Baptist. *8vo, pp.* 24, *half green morocco.* 125

Philadelphia: Printed and Sold by B. FRANKLIN, and D. HALL, (1755)

463 SMITH, WILLIAM. Discourse concerning the *Conversion* of the *Heathen Americans*, and the final Propagation of *Christianity* and the Sciences to the Ends of the Earth. In Two Parts. *8vo, pp.* 53.

Philadelphia, 1760

464 SMITH, WILLIAM. An Oration in Memory of GENERAL MONTGOMERY, and of the *Officers* and *Soldiers* who *Fell* with *Him*, December 31, 1775, Before QUEBEC: Drawn up (and Delivered, February 19th, 1776) at the Desire of the *Honorable Continental Congress.* *8vo, pp.* 44, *uncut.* *Rare.* Philadelphia, 1776

Stained.

465 SMITH, WILLIAM. [The Same.]
Second Edition.
8vo, pp. 36, *uncut.* *Fine, clean copy.*
Philadelphia, Printed; London, Reprinted, 1776

Morrell, half morocco, $4.00. Roche, $3.00.

466 SMITH, WILLIAM. Works of William Smith, D. D., Late Provost of the College and Academy of Philadelphia. *Fine Portrait, engraved by Edwin after Stuart.* *2 vols.* *8vo, boards, uncut,* Philadelphia, 1803

467 SMYTH, J. F. D. TOUR IN THE UNITED STATES of America; Containing An Account of the Present Situation of that Country. Anecdotes of several Members of the CONGRESS, and *General Officers* in the American Army, with Description of the *Indian Nations*, etc., etc. 2 *vols.* *8vo, half Russia.* London, 1784

"Mr. Smyth was an European who went to America to try his fortune as a planter. During the war he leagued with the government, and the zeal of loyalty proved the destruction of his property."

Fisher, $3.38 per vol. Bruce, $2.38 per vol.

468 [Snowden, Richard.] The History of the American Revolution: In Scripture Style. To which is added the Declaration of Independence, the Constitution of the United States of America, and the interesting Farewell Address of General Washington. *Curious and rare Woodcut Portrait of Washington.* 12*mo, full brown crushed levant morocco, gilt back and edges, inside borders of gold, by Bedford. Fine, clean copy; excessively rare.* Frederick County, Md., 1823

Morrell, calf, uncut, $10. Fisher, half calf, uncut, $8.50.

469 [Snowden, Richard.] The Same. *Half crimson morocco, by Matthews.* Clinton, O., 1815

470 Snowden, Richard. The Columbiad; or a Poem on the American War, in Thirteen Cantos. 12*mo, half morocco.* Baltimore, n. d.

471 Souldier's Pocket Bible: Containing the most (if not all) those places contained in Holy Scripture, which doe shew the qualifications of his inner man, that is a fit Souldier to fight the Lords Battels, etc.

An Exact Reprint of the Original Edition of 1643, with a Prefatory Note by George Livermore. *Beautiful Portrait of Oliver Cromwell inserted. Square* 12*mo, boards, uncut.*

Privately Printed. *Rare.* Cambridge, 1861

Morrell, $5.00. Roche, $3.50.

472 South Carolina. Historical Collections of South Carolina; embracing many Rare and Valuable Pamphlets, and other Documents relating to the *History of that State,* from its First Discovery to its Independence, in the year 1776.

Compiled with various Notes and an Introduction by B. R. Carroll. *Map.* 2 *vols.* 8*vo, cloth.* New York, 1836

Fisher, half morocco, $3.12 per vol.

473 South Carolina. Sketch of the History of South Carolina to the close of the Proprietary Government by the Revolution of 1719. With an *Appendix* containing many valuable Records hitherto unpublished. *8vo, pp.* 470, *cloth.* Charleston, 1856

474 Sparks, Jared. Library of American Biography. Conducted by Jared Sparks. *Both Series complete. Engraved Title pages, with Vignette Portraits, etc.*

Original Edition. 25 *vols.* 12*mo, boards, uncut. Scarce.* Boston, 1834–1848

Bruce, half morocco, $1.20 per vol. Fisher, $1.12 per vol. Roche, 87 cents per vol.

475 Sparks, Jared. Life of Gouverneur Morris, with Selections from his Correspondence and Miscellaneous Papers; detailing Events in the American Revolution, the French Revolution, and in the Political History of the United States. *Portrait.* 3 *vols.*, 8*vo, boards, uncut.* Boston, 1832

Wight, $3.50 per vol. Morrell, $1.25 per vol. Bruce, $1.25 per vol.

476 Sparks, Jared. Life and Treason of Benedict Arnold. *Engraved Title, with Portrait.* 12*mo, cloth, uncut.* Boston, 1835

Fisher, half morocco, $2.75. Morrell, $2.00.

477 Stamp Act. A Collection of Pamphlets Relating to the Stamp Act in America. "An Authentic Account of the Proceedings of the *Congress* held at *New York* in 1765, on the Subject of the *American Stamp Act.* 8*vo, pp.* 37, 1767." "Vindication of the *British Colonies.* By *James Otis.* 8*vo, pp.* 48, 1769." "Examination of *Doctor Benjamin Franklin*, relative to the *Repeal* of the *American Stamp Act*, in 1766. 8vo, pp. 50, 1767." "An Enquiry into the Rights of the *British Colonies*, etc., By *Richard Bland*, of Virginia.

8vo, pp. 23, 1769," etc., etc. 4 *vols. 8vo, half bound. Rare.* London, 1766–69

478 STANSBURY AND ODELL. The Loyal Verses of Joseph Stansbury and Doctor Jonathan Odell; Relating to the American Revolution. Edited by Winthrop Sargent. *Autograph letter of the Editor inserted. Small 4to, uncut.* Munsell, Albany, 1860

LIMITED EDITION. Munsell's Historical Series, No. 6.

Fowle, half morocco, $20.00. Wight, half morocco, $12.25. Roche, $12.00. Bruce, morocco, $12.00.

479 ST. CLAIR, MAJOR GENERAL. Narrative of the Manner in which the Campaign against the *Indians*, in the year 1791, was conducted, under the Command of Major General St. Clair, etc. *Portrait and Autograph Document signed*, 1784, *of Gen. St. Clair inserted. 8vo boards, uncut, rough edges.* Philadelphia, 1812

Morrell, $7.25. Wight, $6.75. Fisher, half morocco, Autograph inserted, $6.50. Bruce, $5.00. Whitmore, $4.50.

480 STEDMAN, CAPT. HISTORY OF THE ORIGIN, PROGRESS AND TERMINATION OF THE AMERICAN WAR. 15 *Maps and Plans.* 2 *vols. 4to, boards, uncut, rough edges. Fine copy; scarce.* London, 1794

"Stedman wrote a History of the American War, an actor in the scene, and a sensible man. He served under Howe, Clinton and Cornwallis, and when the conduct of the war is to be estimated, he must be consulted."—*Smythe.*

"The work is also particularly valuable on account of the large and splendid military maps and surveys from the official originals by the British engineering staff, with which it is adorned."

Morrell, 19.00 per vol. Fisher, half morocco, uncut, $19.00 per vol. Bruce, morocco, uncut, $13.50 per vol. Roche, half calf, $8.50 per vol.

481 STEVENS, HENRY. Historical Nuggets. Bibliotheca Americana, or a Descriptive Account of my Collection of Rare Books relating to America. 2 *vols. post 8vo, cloth, gilt top, uncut.*

Limited Edition. *Rare.* *Chiswick Press,* London, 1862

A great portion of this valuable work was destroyed by fire in New York in 1864.

Roche, $10.00 per vol. Morrell, $8.00 per vol. Whitmore, $7.00 per vol.

482 Stiles, Ezra. History of Three of the Judges of King Charles I. Major-General Whalley, Major-General Goffe, and Colonel Dixwell; who, at the Restoration, 1860, fled to America; and were secreted and concealed, in Massachusetts and Connecticut, for nearly thirty years, etc. *Portrait, (fine impression) and plates.* 12*mo.* *Original sheep binding.* *Fine, clean copy: rare.* Hartford, 1794

View of the Judges' cave, West Rock, New Haven, inserted.

Morrell, morocco, $20. H. A. Smith, $15. Wight, $12. Fisher, $11.50. Bruce, $11.50.

483 Stith, William. The History of the First Discovery and Settlement of Virginia; being a Essay towards a General History of this Colony. With an Appendix to the First Part of the History of Virginia: containing a Collection of such Ancient Charters or Letters Patent, as relate to that Period of Time, and are still extant in our Publick Offices in the *Capitol,* or in other Authentic Papers and Records. 8*vo, full polished calf, gilt back and edges.*

Williamsburgh: Printed by William Parks, 1747

Beautiful copy, with good margins and having both Title pages. Very rare.

H. A. Smith, $35. Whitmore, $31. Morrell, $31.

484 Stith, William. History of the First Discovery and Settlement of Virginia. *Thick Roy.* 8*vo, uncut.*

Large Paper: *Only* 50 *copies printed.*

New York—Reprinted for Joseph Sabin, 1865

This valuable reprint is a perfect fac-simile of the above rare Williamsburgh edition.

Roche, $9.00.

485 STOBO. Memoirs of Major Robert Stobo, of the Virginia Regiment. *Map.* 16*mo, cloth.*
Pittsburgh, 1854

486 STONE, WILLIAM L. Tales and Sketches,—such as they are—2 *vols.* 12*mo, cloth.* New York, 1834

Among the romances contained in these volumes—are, "The Grave of the Indian King," "Lake St. Sacrament," etc.

487 STONE, WILLIAM L. The Poetry and History of Wyoming: containing Campbell's Gertrude, with a Biographical Sketch of the Author, by Washington Irving, etc. *Plates,* 12*mo, cloth.* New York, 1841

Some copies were issued without the plates.
Morrell, half morocco, uncut, $3.50.

488 STONE, WILLIAM L. Poetry and History of Wyoming: containing Campbell's Gertrude, and the History of Wyoming from its Discovery to the beginning of the present century. Third Edition, with an Index. *Portraits of Campbell, Col. Brandt, and Plates by Westall inserted. Thick* 12*mo. Half green morocco, gilt top, uncut.* Albany, 1864

489 STONE, WM. L. Life of Joseph Brant (Thayendanega), including the Border Wars of the American Revolution, and Sketches of the Indian Campaigns of Generals Harmar, St. Clair, and Wayne, etc. *Portraits.* 2 *vols. royal* 8*vo, uncut.*
LARGE PAPER; *only* 50 *copies printed.* Albany, 1864

Morrell, $5.00 per vol. Roche, $3.00 per vol.

490 STONE, WM. L. Life and Times of Sir William Johnson, Bart. *Portraits.* 2 *vols. Royal* 8*vo, uncut.*
LARGE PAPER: *only* 50 *copies printed.* Albany, 1865

Roche, $3.00 per vol.

491 STONE, WM. L. Life and Times of Sa-go-ye-wat-ha, or Red Jacket. With a Memoir of the Author by his Son.

Portraits of the Author, and Red Jacket, etc. Roy. 8vo, uncut.

LARGE PAPER: *Only* 50 *copies printed.* Albany, 1866

Roche, $7.00.

492 STONE, WM. L. [The Same.] *Portraits on India paper, etc., 4to, uncut.*

BUT 10 COPIES PRINTED THIS SIZE. *Scarce.*

Albany, 1866

Accompanying this volume is an original Autograph letter, (of great historical interest,) of PRESIDENT JEFFERSON *written to* "BROTHER HANDSOME LAKE," *Washington, Nov.* 3, 1802. 3 *pp.* 4*to, deprecating the use of spirituous liquor among them, advocating their right to sell their lands, etc.*

493 STRENGTH OUT OF WEAKNESSE; Or, a Glorious Manifestation Of the further Progresse of the Gospel among the *Indians* in New-England. Held forth in Sundry Letters from divers Ministers and others to the Corporation established by Parliament for Promoting the Gospel among the Heathen in *New-England, etc.* Formerly set forth by Mr. *Henry Whitfield,* late Pastor of *Gilford,* in *New-England. Small* 4*to, full purple levant morocco, gilt, by Bedford. Very fine copy. Rare.* London, 1652

This valuable little tract contains letters from John Eliot, William Leverich, Thomas Mayhew, etc.

Morrell, $30.

494 STRONG, THOMAS M. History of the Towu of Flatbush, in Kings County, Long Island. Published by Request. *Map and Plates.* 12*mo, cloth.* New York, 1842

Morrell, $4.00.

495 STUART, J. W. Life of Captain Nathan Hale, the Martyr-Spy of the American Revolution. Second Edition. Enlarged and Improved. *Plates.* 12*mo, cloth.*

Hartford, 1856

Wight, $5.75. Morrell, $2.63.

496 SULLIVAN'S CAMPAIGN. Notices of; or, the Revolutionary Warfare in Western New York. *Plate, representing the "Hill of the Revolutionary Patriots at Mt. Hope, Rochester."* 12*mo*, *cloth*. *Scarce.*

Rochester, 1842

Published "pursuant to a resolution adopted by the people assembled in Livingston County, to preserve a record of the honors paid to the soldiers whose blood first consecrated to freedom the soil of the Genessee Valley."

Morrell, $4.00. Roche, half morocco, $3.25.

497 SUTCLIFF, ROBERT. Travels in some parts of North America, in the years 1804, 1805, and 1806. *View of Niagara Falls.* 12*mo*, *boards*, *uncut*, *rough edges*. *Rare.*

Philadelphia, 1812

498 SWETT, S. History of Bunker Hill Battle. With a Plan. Third Edition, with Notes. *Portraits of Gens. Warren, Putnam, and other plates inserted.* 8*vo*, *half Purple morocco*, *gilt top*, *uncut*. Boston, 1827

499 SWETT, S. [The Same.] *Plan.* 8*vo*, *uncut*.

Boston, 1827

TALLMADGE, COL. BENJAMIN. Memoir, prepared by Himself, at the request of his Children. *Fine portrait after Col. Trumbull.* 8*vo*, *pp.* 70, *cloth*.
PRIVATELY PRINTED. *Very scarce.* *New York*, 1858

This was strictly a privately printed volume, and seldom occurs for sale, not half a dozen copies having been offered at public auction since its issue, and is consequently almost unattainable. It is a curious fact that the prices quoted below are for but one copy, that of Messrs. Morrell, Whitmore and Davis being identically the same.

Morrell, $10.00. Davis, $7.50. Whitmore, $6.00.

501 TARLETON, LIEUT. COL. History of the Campaign of 1780 and 1781 in the southern Provinces of North America. *Map and plans.* 4*to*, *boards*, *uncut*, *rough edges*.

London, 1787

Fine copy. Rare and beautiful full length, portrait of Col. Tarleton inserted.

"Colonel Tarleton's history gives a minute detail of all the military operations in both Carolinas, and part of Virginia, until the surrender of Lord Cornwallis with his whole army at Yorktown, Oct. 19, 1781."—*Rich.*

Morrell, $20.00. Bruce, half morocco, $20.00. Roche, $11.50.

502 TARLETON. STRICTURES ON LIEUT. COL. TARLETON'S HISTORY "of the campaign of 1780 and 1781, in the Southern Provinces of North America," wherein Military Characters and Corps are vindicated from injurious aspersions, and several important Transactions placed in their proper point of view. In a series of Letters to a Friend, by RODERICK MACKENZIE late Lieutenant in the 71st Regiment. To which is added a DETAIL OF THE SIEGE OF NINETY-SIX, AND THE RE-CAPTURE OF THE ISLAND OF NEW PROVIDENCE. *Portrait of Col. Tarleton inserted.* 8*vo, pp.* 186, *boards, uncut, rough edges. Fine clean copy. Very rare.*

London, Printed for the AUTHOR 1787

503 TEA-PARTY. RETROSPECT OF THE BOSTON TEA-PARTY. With a Memoir of George R. T. Hewes, a Survivor of the little Band of Patriots who drowned the Tea in Boston Harbour, in 1773. By a Citizen of New York. *Portrait of Hewes.* 12*mo, boards, uncut.*

New York, 1834

Unusual wide margins, having the appearance of a large paper copy; can trace no similar copy.

Morrell, trimmed, with Portrait, etc. inserted, $6.00.

504 TEA-PARTY. Traits of the Tea-Party; being a Memoir of *George R. T. Hewes*, one of the last of its Survivors; with a *History of that Transaction;* Reminiscences of the Massacre and the Siege, and other Stories of Old Times. By a Bostonian. *Etched Portrait of Hewes. Rare Engraving of the "Destruction of Tea in Boston Harbor" inserted.* 12*mo, cloth, uncut.*

New York, 1835

Fisher, calf, Autograph inserted, $6.50.

505 THACHER, JAMES. Military Journal during the American Revolutionary War, from 1775 to 1783, describing Interesting Events and Transactions of this Period; with Numerous Historical Facts and Anecdotes, from the Original Manuscript. To which is added, An Appendix, Containing Biographical Sketches of several General Officers. Second Edition, revised and corrected. *8vo, boards, uncut. Fine copy, with rough edges. Scarce.* Boston, 1827

H. A. Smith, $4.25.

506 THACHER, JAMES. [The same.]
FIRST EDITION. *8vo, uncut, rough edges. A number of Plates inserted, Lady Ackland, Lord Stirling, Gens. Sullivan, Putnam, etc.* Boston, 1823

Whitmore, no plates, $16.00. Morrell, Portrait inserted, $7.00. Roche, no plates, $4.50.

507 THACHER, JAMES. American Medical Biography; or, Memoirs of Eminent Physicians who have flourished in America. To which is prefixed a Succinct History of Medical Science in the United States, from the first Settlement of the Country. *Portraits. 2 vols. 8vo, boards, uncut.* Boston, 1828

Contains Portraits of Drs. Thacher, John Bard, Samuel Bard, etc. Fine impressions.
Fisher, 2 vols. in 1, half morocco, $ 17.00. Roche, *Fisher's copy*, $7.00. Morrell, 2 vol s,in 1, $7.00. Whitmore, 2 vols. in 1, $5.50. H. A. Smith, $3.00 per vol.

508 THOMAS, GABRIEL. An Historical and Geographical Account of the Province and Country of Pennsilvania; and of West-New-Jersey in America, etc., etc. With a Map of both Countries. By Gabriel Thomas who resided there about Fifteen Years. *Portrait of William Penn inserted, also very rare print from the Columbian Magazine of "Paysaick Falls," New Jersey.*

Printed on blue paper. Folio, Full Morocco, gilt edges. London, 1698

LARGE PAPER. New YORK, 1848

Of this very rare fac-simile reprint (by H. A. Brady, Esq., in 1848), but 10 copies were issued on large paper.
Morrell, $20.00.

509 THOMAS, GABRIEL. An Historical and Geographical Account of the Province and Country of Pensilvania and West-New-Jersey in America, etc. With a Map of both Countries. *Map. Fac-simile of the Original,* (London, 1698), *lithographed by Henry Austin Brady.* 12*mo. Half levant morocco, gilt top, uncut.*
New York, 1848

Fisher, $2.38. Roche, cloth, $2.00. H. A. Smith, cloth, $2.00.

510 THOMPSON, BENJAMIN F. History of Long Island; from its Discovery and Settlement, to the Present Time, With many Important and Interesting Matters, etc. Second Edition, revised and greatly enlarged, *Portrait of the Author, and Plates.* 2 *vols.* 8*vo, cloth, uncut.* New York, 1843
Scarce in uncut condition.

Morrell, $6.00 per vol. Roche, $4.12 per vol.

511 TICKNOR, GEORGE. Life of William Hickling Prescott. With a Prefatory Notice, an Appendix, and an Index. *Illustrated with a Portrait, an engraving of the Bust, by Greenough, and beautiful woodcuts, including numerous ornamental head and tail pieces and initials.* 2 *additional Portraits inserted. Small* 4*to vellum cloth, uncut.*
LIMITED EDITION: *beautifully printed.* Boston, 1864

Fowle, half morocco, $10.00. Whitmore, $7.00. Morrell, Autograph, etc., inserted, $7.00.

512 TREATY, HELD AT THE TOWN OF LANCASTER, in Pennsylvania, by the Honourable the Lieutenant-Governor of the

Province, and the Honourable the Commissioners for the Provinces of *Virginia and Maryland, with the Indians of the Six Nations, in June,* 1744. *Folio, pp.* 39. *Half Morocco, gilt top, uncut. Philadelphia: Printed and sold by B. Franklin, at the New-Printing Office, near the Market.* 1744

In fine condition. The extreme rarity of this work can be readily imagined, when but TWO *copies, including the above, are the only ones known to have been offered for sale in this city.*

Morrell, calf, $40.00. Roche, *Morrell's copy,* $30.00. Wight, *copy now offered,* $20.00.

513 TRIAL. A Brief NARRATIVE of the CASE and TRIAL of JOHN PETER ZENGER, Printer of the NEW YORK WEEKLY JOURNAL. *Folio, pp.* 39. *Full purple levant morocco, rich, inside borders, by Matthews.*

NEW YORK Printed: LANCASTER Re-printed, and Sold by W. DUNLAP, at the *New Printing Office*, in *Queen Street*, 1756

514 TRIAL. *Proceedings* of a *General Court Martial*, Held at Brunswick, in the State of New Jersey, by Order of His Excellency GENERAL WASHINGTON, Commander in Chief of the Army of the United States of America, For the *Trial* of MAJOR GENERAL LEE, July 4th, 1778. Major General Lord Stirling, President. *Rare old Mezzotint Portrait, fine impression of Gen. Charles Lee inserted. Folio, pp.* 62. *Full purple levant morocco, rich, inside borders, by Matthews.*

PHILADELPHIA: *Printed* by *John Dunlap*, in Market Street. MDCCLXXVIII

515 TRIAL. *Proceedings* of a *General Court Martial*, Held at *White Plains*, in the State of *New York*, by Order of his Excellency *General Washington*, Commander in Chief of the Army of the United States of America, For the *Trial* of MAJOR GENERAL ST. CLAIR, August 25, 1778. Major General Lincoln, President. *Plan of*

Mount Independence, Forts, etc. Portrait of General St. Clair inserted. Folio, pp. 52. Full purple levant morocco, rich inside borders, by Matthews.

PHILADELPHIA: Printed by HALL and SELLERS, in Market Street, MDCCLXXVIII

516 TRIAL. PROCEEDINGS of a GENERAL COURT MARTIAL, Held at *Major General* LINCOLN's Quarters Near *Quaker Hill*, in the State of New York, by Order of his Excellency GENERAL WASHINGTON, Commander in Chief of the Army of the United States of America, for the *Trial* of MAJOR GENERAL SCHUYLER, October 1, 1778. *Major General* LINCOLN, *President. Portrait of General Schuyler inserted. Folio, pp. 62. Full purple levant morocco, rich inside borders, by Matthews.*

PHILADELPHIA: Printed by HALL and SELLERS, in Market Street. MDCCLXXVIII

IT IS NOT KNOWN THAT THE ABOVE FOUR TRIALS ARE CONTAINED IN ANY OTHER COLLECTION, AND IN ALL PROBABILITY BUT FEW POSSESS ANY ONE OF THEM.

THEY ARE ALL BOUND UNIFORM. ARE IN FINE CONDITION, AND OF EXCESSIVE RARITY.

517 TRIAL. Alton Trials: of Winthrop S. Gilman, who was indicted with Enoch Long, Amos B. Roff, and others, for the *Crime of Riot*, committed on the night of the 7th of November, 1837, while engaged in defending a *Printing Press*, from an attack made on it at that time, by an *Armed* Mob, etc., etc. *Plate of the Riot at Alton, Illinois. 12mo, cloth.* New York, 1838

518 TRIAL. BOSTON MASSACRE:—The Trial of William Wemms, James Hartegan, Wm. M'Cauley, Hugh White, Matthew Killroy, William Warren, John Carrol, and Hugh Montgomery, Soldiers in his Majesty's 29th Regiment of Foot, *for the Murder of Crispus Attucks, Samuel Gray, Samuel Maverick, James Caldwell and Patrick Carr, on Monday Evening, the 5th of March*, 1770, at

the Superior Court, Held at Boston, the 27th Day of November, 1770, etc. *8vo, pp.* 216, *boards, uncut, rough edges.*

Boston, Printed, London, reprinted, 1770

Fine, clean copy: of excessive rarity in uncut condition.

Bruce, half morocco, $11.00.

519 TRIAL. BURR. Reports of the Trials of Colonel Aaron Burr (late Vice-President of the United States), for Treason and for a Misdemeanor, in preparing the means of a Military Expedition against Mexico, a Territory of the King of Spain, with whom the United States were at Peace, etc., etc. By David Robertson. *Portrait of Burr inserted.* 2 *vols. 8vo, half green morocco, rich gilt back, gilt top, uncut, by Matthews. Fine, clean copy. Very rare.* Philadelphia, 1808

One of the choicest copies ever offered for sale.

See BURR for quotations of prices.

520 TRIAL. GALLOWAY. Examination of *Joseph Galloway, Esq.*, Late Speaker of the House of Assembly of Pennsylvania. Before the House of Commons, in a Committee on the *American Papers.* With Explanatory Notes. *8vo, pp.* 85. *Half green morocco.*

London, 1779

Wight, $4.00.

521 TRIAL. HARMAR. Proceedings of a Court of Enquiry, Held at the special Request of Brigadier-General JOSIAH HARMAR, to investigate his Conduct as Commanding Officer of the *Expedition* against the *Miami Indians*, 1790: the same having been transmitted by Major-General St. Clair, to the Secretary of the United States, etc. Published by Authority. *Fine Portrait on India paper of Gen. Harmar inserted, also Autograph note signed "Jos. Harmar," August 29th,* 1789. *Folio, pp.* 31. *Half calf, uncut.* Philadelphia, 1791

Very scarce, the present copy being the same one formerly in the collections of Messrs. Roche and Wight. The Autograph has since been inserted.

Roche, $13.00. Wight, $8.00.

522 TRIAL. HENLEY, COL. DAVID. PROCEEDINGS OF A COURT MARTIAL held at Cambridge by order of *Maj. Gen. Heath*, commanding the American Troops, for the Trial of *Colonel David Henley*, accused by *General Burgoyne*, of ill-treatment of the British Soldiers, etc. *Rare old Portrait of Gen. Burgoyne inserted.* 8*vo, half purple morocco, gilt top, uncut edges. Fine copy, very scarce.* London, 1778

Bruce, no portrait, $6.00.

523 TRIAL. HORSMANDEN, DANIEL. The New York conspiracy; or, a History of the Negro Plot, with the Journal of the Proceedings against the Conspirators at New York in the years 1741–2. 8*vo, half green morocco, gilt top, uncut.* New York, 1810

Excessively rare in uncut condition. Has inserted a valuable Historical Document signed by CHIEF-JUSTICE HORSMANDEN, *dated New York, April* 26, 1759.

Bruce, boards, uncut, $26.00. Wight, half morocco, trimmed, $9.00. Morrell, half sheep, trimmed, $9.00.

524 TRIAL. LEE. Proceedings of a General Court-Martial held at Brunswick, in the State of New Jersey, by Order of General Washington, for the trial of MAJOR-GENERAL LEE, *July 4th*, 1778, *Major-General Lord Stirling, President. Rare and beautiful Portrait of General Lee inserted.* 8*vo, half green morrocco, gilt top, uncut.*

PRIVATELY REPRINTED. 100 *copies.* New York, 1864

H. A. Smith, unbound, $10.00.

525 TRIAL. ZENGER. The Trial of *John Peter Zenger* of New York, Printer, who was lately Try'd and Acquitted for Printing and Publishing a Libel against the Govern-

ment. With the Pleadings and Arguments on both Sides. *Small 4to, green morocco, extra, gilt top, uncut, by Matthews.*

FIRST LONDON EDITION. *Scarce.* London, 1738

Morrell, half morocco, trimmed, $6.50.

526 TRIAL. WEBSTER. Report of the Case of John W. Webster for the murder of George Parkman—with the hearing on the Petition for a Writ of Error, the Prisoner's Confessional Statements, and Application for Commutation of Sentence, &c. By George Bemis, one of the Counsel in the Case. *Numerous engravings, plans, fac-similes of letters, &c. Thick royal 8vo, pp.* 628. *Cloth, uncut. Scarce.* Boston, 1850

Rare Autograph Letter, 1 *page 4to, Boston, April* 23, 1819, *of* PROFESSOR WEBSTER *inserted, also Card of Admission to Lectures on Chemistry at Harvard University, signed by him, with Portraits of* DR. PARKMAN *and* PROFESSOR WEBSTER.

The most faithful account of "one of the darkest incidents in legal or human annals."

Bruce, half morocco, $4.50.

527 TRIAL. ANDRÉ. Proceedings of a *Board* of General Officers, Held by Order of His Excellency *Gen. Washington* Commander in Chief of the Army of the United States of America, Respecting *Major* JOHN ANDRÉ, Adjutant General of the British Army, September 29, 1780. *8vo, pp.* 21, *half morocco, uncut.* ORIGINAL EDITION. *Fine copy, very scarce.*

Philadelphia, 1780

Inserted in this copy is the full length portrait of Major Andre, choice original impression well known to be of excessive variety.

Roche, $37.50. Morrell, morocco, $26.00.

528 TRUMBULL, BENJAMIN. Complete History of Connecticut, Civil and Ecclesiastical, from the Emigration of its First Planters from England, in the year 1630, to the

year 1764; and to the close of the Indian Wars. *Portrait, fine impression.* 2 *vols.* 8*vo, sheep.*

New Haven, 1818

Beautiful copy.
Wight, half morocco, $5.50 per vol. Morrell, $5.00 per vol.

529 TRUMBULL, HENRY. History of the Discovery of America; of the Landing of our Forefathers at Plymouth, and of their most remarkable *Engagements with the Indians in New England*, from their first landing in 1620, until the final Subjugation of the Natives in 1679, etc., etc. *Plates.* 8*vo, boards, uncut, rough edges. Rare in uncut condition.* Boston, 1828

530 TRUMBULL, JOHN. McFINGAL: a Modern Epic Poem, in Four Cantos. *Portrait inserted.* 12*mo. Full crimson levant morocco, gilt back and edges, inside borders, by Bedford.*

FIRST EDITION. *Very rare.* Hartford, 1782

Beautiful copy, with large margins.
Morrell, $7.00.

531 TRUMBULL, JOHN. Poetical Works, Containing *McFingal*, a Modern Epic Poem, revised and corrected, with copious Explanatory Notes, etc., and a collection of Poems on various subjects written before and during the Revolutionary War. *Portrait and Plates by Tisdale, with fine extra portrait inserted.* 2 *vols.* 8*vo, half green morocco, gilt top, uncut.* Hartford, 1820

Whitmore, same copy, $3.00 per vol.

532 TRUMBULL, JOHN. McFingal. An Epic Poem. With Introduction and Notes, by Benson J. Lossing. *Tinted paper. Portrait. Royal* 8*vo, pp.* 322, *cloth, uncut.*
LARGE PAPER: *only* 100 *Copies printed.*

New York, 1860

Fowle, half morocco, $10.00. Fisher, $7.00. Wight, $6.25. Morrell, $5.00. Roche, $3.50. Whitmore, $3.50.

533 TRUMBULL, JOHN. Autobiography, Reminiscences and Letters, from 1756 to 1841. *Fine Portrait, Maps and Etchings. Extended to* TWO VOLUMES *and illustrated by the insertion of* 95 *Plates, very many fine and rare, together with Autograph Letter of* COL. TRUMBULL, *July* 17*th*, 1829. 2 *vols.* 8*vo, full brown morocco, gilt, gilt top, uncut, by Matthews.* New York, 1841

Allan, 2 vols. morocco, extra plates, $80.00 per vol. Morrell, in one vol. half morocco, extra plates, $25.00.

534 TRUMBULL, JOHN. [The Same]. *Portrait, Maps and Etchings.* 8*vo, cloth, uncut.* New York, 1841

Fisher, half morocco, Autograph Letter inserted, $7.00. Whitmore, $4.00.

535 TUCKER, GEORGE. Life of Thomas Jefferson, Third President of the United States, with Parts of his Correspondence never before published, etc. *Portrait. Fine Autograph Letter of the Author, with extra Portrait of Jefferson inserted.* 2 *vols.* 8*vo, half morocco, gilt top, uncut. Fine clean copy.* Philadelphia, 1837

Morrell, cloth, $2.00 per vol.

536 TUDOR, WILLIAM. Life of James Otis, of Massachusetts; containing also, Notices of some Contemporary Characters and Events from the year 1760 to 1775. *Fine Portrait engraved by Durand, and other plates. Rare Original Document signed by* JAMES OTIS, *with seven lines in his handwriting, August* 28*th*, 1764, *inserted. Thick,* 8*vo, boards, uncut, rough edges. Cover loose. Fine copy. Scarce.* Boston, 1823

Morrell, half morocco, extra plates, $11.00. Fowle, $7.00. Wight, $5.25. Whitmore, $3.25.

537 TUDOR, WILLIAM. Letters on the Eastern States. *Second and best Edition.* 8*vo, boards, uncut, rough edges.* Boston, 1821

UPHAM, CHARLES W. Salem Witchcraft; with an Account of Salem Village, and a History of Opinions on Witchcraft and kindred subjects. *Plates and fac-similes. 2 vols. 8vo, cloth, uncut.*

TINTED PAPER. Boston, 1867

VAN SCHAACK, HENRY C. Life of Peter Van Schaack, LL.D., embracing Selections from his Correspondence and other Writings, during the *American Revolution*, and his Exile in England. By his Son. *Fine Portrait. 8vo, cloth, uncut.* New York, 1842

540 VAN SCHAACK, HENRY C. Henry Cruger; the Colleague of Edmund Burke in the British Parliament. A Paper read before the New York Historical Society, January 4th, 1859. *Beautiful Portrait, tinted, of Henry Cruger inserted. 8vo.* New York, 1859

541 VIRGINIA. The Proceedings of the HOUSE OF BURGESSES of VIRGINIA, Convened in General Assembly, on *Thursday*, the first day of *June*, 1775, will fully appear in their Journals, printed at large; but as it was judged necessary that the most material transactions should be seen in one connected and distinct point of view, the House ordered that these should be published in a pamphlet, and they are contained in the following sheets. *4to, pp. 48. Of excessive rarity.*

Williamsburg: Printed by ALEXANDER PURDIE, (1775)

Fine copy, in nearly uncut condition.

542 VOYAGES. DAMPIER, CAPTAIN WILLIAM. New Voyage around the World. Describing particularly the *Isthmus* of *America*, several Coasts and Islands in the *West Indies*, the Isles of *Cape Verde*, etc., etc., their Soil, Rivers, Harbours, Plants, Fruits, Animals, and Inhabitants. Their Customs, Religion, Government, Trade, etc. *Numerous Maps. 3 vols. 8vo, calf.*

London, 1705–09–17

543 VOYAGES. Early Voyages up and down the Mississippi, by Cavelin, St. Cosme, Le Sueur, Gravier, and Guignas. With an Introduction, Notes and Index. By John Gilmary Shea. *Small 4to, half crimson morocco, gilt top, uncut.*

MUNSELL'S HISTORICAL SERIES, NO. 8. Albany, 1861
Limited Edition.

544 VOYAGES. IRVING, WASHINGTON. History of the Life and Voyages of Christopher Columbus. *Maps. Fine Portraits of Irving, and Columbus inserted. 4 vols. 8vo, boards, uncut.*

MURRAY'S FINE LARGE TYPE EDITION. London, 1828

545 VOYAGES. WAFER, LIONEL. New Voyage and Description of the *Isthmus* of *America*, Giving an Account of the AUTHOR'S Abode there, the *Form* and *Make* of the *Country*, etc. The *Indian Inhabitants*, their Features, Complexion, etc. *Curious Plates, and Map. 8vo, pp.* 224. *Full polished calf, gilt back and edges, by Pratt. Beautiful copy.* London, 1699

WALKER, SIR HOVENDEN. Journal; or full Account of the late Expedition to *Canada*, with an Appendix, containing Commissions, Orders, Instructions, etc., etc., relating thereto. *8vo, full green levant morocco, gilt edges. Fine copy.* London, 1720

"Sir Hovenden Walker was the naval commander of the great expedition against Canada, which sailed from Boston, N. E., in the summer of 1711; but which proved a complete failure, owing to the unskilfulness of the pilots, by which eight ships and nearly one thousand men were lost in the river St. Lawrence. Great blame was attached to Sir Hovenden, and he published this account in his own vindication."—*Nichols' Lit. Anecdotes.*

547 WALLABOUT PRISON SHIP. Account of the Interment of the Remains of AMERICAN PATRIOTS, who perished on board the British Prison Ships during the American

Revolution. *With Notes and an Appendix*, by Henry R. Stiles, M. D. *Plate. Portraits of Dr. Mitchill, Dewitt Clinton and Jefferson inserted.* 8vo, *uncut. Only* 80 *copies printed.* New York, 1865

Beautifully printed, with characteristic head and tail pieces.

548 WALLACE, JOHN WILLIAM. An Address delivered at the Celebration by the New York Historical Society, May 20, 1863, of the *Two Hundredth Birth Day* of Mr. WILLIAM BRADFORD who introduced the Art of Printing into the Middle Colonies of British America. 12 *Plates inserted, including View of Bradford's Tombstone in Trinity Churchyard, Portraits of Franklin, George Bancroft and Gulian C. Verplanck,* (*proofs*,) *George Fox, Cotton Mather, William Penn, Attorney-General Bradford, etc., with an original title page from the* "LEED'S ALMANAC," *having* BRADFORD'S *imprint, New York,* 1735, *also Autograph Letter of the Author.* 8vo, *half green crushed levant morocco, gilt top, uncut.*

LIMITED EDITION. Albany, 1863

This copy also contains the fac-similes.

549 WALLACK. Memorial. Sketch of the Life of James William Wallack, (Senior,) Late Actor and Manager. *Vignette Portrait. Beautiful Portrait on India paper inserted.* 4to.

LARGE PAPER: 50 *copies printed.*

New York, T. H. Morrell, 1865

550 WALLACK. Memorial. [The Same.] *Vignette Portrait. Roy.* 8vo,

200 *copies printed.* New York, T. H. Morrell, 1865

551 WALTON AND COTTON'S COMPLETE ANGLER. Pickering's splendid edition, edited by Sir Harris Nichols, illustrated by Stothard, Inskipp, etc., original copy, *with*

early impressions of the plates, and a duplicate set of proofs before letters on India paper, 4 thick vols. colombier size, bound by Riviere in his best style, green levant morocco extra, the sides and back enriched with beautiful gold tooling, gilt edges.

London, Pickering, 1836

UNIQUE COPY illustrated and extended into 4 thick volumes royal octavo, by the addition of 240 extra plates consisting of Portraits, Views, Fish, and Fishing Subjects, mostly fine proofs, and all early impressions. Many of the Portraits, etc., are rare, including some by Hollar, etc. This copy has been illustrated *con amore* with the greatest care, and in the most complete manner. There are four extra titles (one to each volume), beautifully executed by hand in pen and ink. The binding and condition of the book is superb, each leaf having a separate guard.

The illustrations inserted in this superb work include many of the choicest specimens of engraving by Bromley, Finden, Pye, Warren, S. W. Reynolds, Worthington, etc., many being proofs in a finished and unfinished state, also beautifully colored plates of various fish, and colored illustrations by Bunbury and others.

Among the portraits are fine and rare ones of Cowley, Dr. Johnson. Lord Bacon, Shakespeare, Queen Elizabeth, Henry VIII., Bunyan, Lilly, Aldrovanus, etc., etc., and including also the excessively rare portrait of WILLIAM PICKERING, publisher, a fine proof on India paper from a private plate, impressions from which are valued in London at about £2.

Mr. John Allan's copy of this work extended to FOUR *volumes, as above, with* 260 *extra plates, green morocco, gilt, sold for* $150 *per vol., or* $600 *for the set.*

552 WALTON AND COTTON'S COMPLETE ANGLER. [The Same.] With copious Notes, for the most part Original, a *Bibliographical Preface*, giving an account of *Fishing and Fishing Books*, from the earliest Antiquity to the time of Walton, etc., etc. *Portraits and Plates. Beautiful Portrait on India paper of Walton inserted. Royal 8vo, half levant morocco, gilt top, uncut.* 1200

LARGE PAPER. 100 *copies printed. Scarce.*

New York, 1847

Edited by the late Dr. Bethune. Contains "the most complete Catalogue of Books on Angling, etc., ever printed."

553 WANSEY, HENRY. Journal of an Excursion to the United States of North America, in the Summer of 1794. *Embellished with the Profile of General Washington, and an Aqua-tinta View of the State House at Philadelphia.* 8vo, *boards, uncut, rough edges. Rare.*
Salisbury, 1796

Curious Portrait of General Washington, taken in 1791.
Bruce, half calf, trimmed, $3.62.

554 WAR, THE. Being a Faithful Record of the Transactions of the War between the United States of America, their Territories, and the United Kingdom of Great Britain and Ireland, and the Dependencies thereof. 45 *Plates inserted, many very scarce, including Portraits of Commodores Lawrence, Perry, Decatur and other Naval Officers, together with Views, Sea-Fights, etc.* 3 *vols. in* 2, 4*to, half green morocco, gilt.*
New York, 1813–14

War Newspaper, edited by Samuel Woodworth.

555 WAR OF 1812. Barbarities of the Enemy, exposed in a Report of the Committee of the House of Representatives of the United States, Appointed to inquire into the spirit and manner in which the war has been waged by the Enemy, with Documents, etc. 12*mo, boards, uncut.* Troy, 1813

556 WARD, NATHANIEL. The Simple Cobler of Aggawamm in America. Willing to help mend his Native Country, lamentably tattered, both in the upper-Leather and sole, with all the honest stitches he can take. And as willing never to bee paid for his work, by Old English wonted pay. *It is his Trade to patch all the year long, gratis.* Therefore I pray Gentlemen keep your purses. By THEODORE DE LA GUARD. *The Third Edition, with some Amendments. Small* 4*to, pp.* 80. *Full polished calf, gilt back and edges, by Pratt. Very rare.*
London, 1647

Clean, and with large margins, and as fine a copy as has ever been offered for sale.

Allan, $55. Roche, $42.50. Bruce, $27. Morrell, morocco, $26.

557 WARD, NATHANIEL. [The Same.] Edited by David Pulsifer. 12*mo, uncut.* London, 1647
REPRINT. Boston, 1843

558 WARNER AND ALLEN. Memoir of COL. SETH WARNER, by *Daniel Chipman, LL.D.* To which is added the Life of COL. ETHAN ALLEN, by *Jared Sparks, LL.D.* 12*mo, cloth.* Middlebury, 1848

559 WASHINGTON. Alsop, Richard. A Poem; Sacred to the Memory of George Washington, late President of the United States, etc. 8*vo, pp.* 23. Hartford, 1800

560 WASHINGTON. Ames, Fisher. An Oration on the Sublime Virtues of General Washington, before his Honor, the Lieutenant-Govenor, the Council, and the two Branches of the Legislature of Massachusetts, etc. 8*vo, pp.* 31, *uncut.* Boston, 1800

Morrell, $7.00.

561 WASHINGTON. BANCROFT, AARON. An Essay on the Life of George Washington, Commander-in-Chief of the American Army through the American War, and the First President of the United States. *Fine Portrait.* 8*vo, full polished calf, gilt back and edges, by Pratt. Beautiful copy. Rare.* Worcester, 1807

Fisher, half morocco, uncut, L. S. of Washington inserted, $35.50.

562 WASHINGTON. BANCROFT, AARON. Life of George Washington, Commander-in-Chief of the American Army through the Revolutionary War, etc. *Letter Signed by Washington,* 1 *p.* 4*to.* "*New Windsor, Dec.* 9, 1780," *inserted.* 8*vo, boards, uncut.*
London, Stockdale, 1808

Wight, $6.50.

563 WASHINGTON. BINNEY, HORACE. An inquiry into the Formation of Washington's Farewell Address. *8vo, cloth.* PRIVATELY PRINTED. Philadelphia, 1859

Wight, half morocco. extra plates. $6.25. Roche, sheets, $3.00. Bruce, $3.00.

564 WASHINGTON. Biographical Memoirs of the Illustrious General George Washington, First President of the United States of America, and Commander-in-Chief of their Armies, during the Revolutionary War. Dedicated to the Youth of America. *Monument with initials "G. W." on title page.* 12*mo, pp.* 103, *boards. Very rare.* Baltimore, 1812

Corner, half calf, $3.75.

565 WASHINGTON. Biographical Memoirs of the Illustrious General George Washington, late President of the United States of America, and Commander-in-Chief of their Armies, during the Revolutionary War. Dedicated to the Youth of America. *Portrait of Washington, angel crowning him with laurels, by Matthews.* 12*mo, pp.* 160, *crimson levant morocco, rich gilt back, and inside borders. Very rare.* Barnard, Vt., 1813

566 WASHINGTON. Biography and Character of George Washington, His Farewell Address to the People of the United States, and the *Federal Constitution*, with the Amendments. *Portrait.* 16*mo, pp.* 105, *morocco, gilt. Scarce. Title page and Portrait mounted.* Concord, 1814

567 WASHINGTON. BLAKE, GEORGE. Masonic Eulogy, on the Life of the Illustrious *Brother George Washington.* pronounced before the Brethren of ST. JOHN'S LODGE, on the evening of the 4th Feb. 5800, etc. By Brother *George Blake.* 8*vo, pp.* 23, *uncut.* Boston, 5800. (1800)

568 WASHINGTON. BUCKMINSTER, JOSEPH. Sermon Preached to the North and South Parishes in Portsmouth, Fraternally united in observance of the 22nd February, 1800, the day appointed by Congress to pay tributary respect to the Memory of *Gen. Washington.* *8vo, pp.* 28. *Scarce.*

Portsmouth, New Hampshire, 1800

569 WASHINGTON. Collection of the *Speeches* of the *President of the United States* to both Houses of Congress, at the Opening of every Session, with their Answers Also the *Addresses* of the President, etc., etc. 12*mo. Sheep.*

Boston, July, 1796

570 WASHINGTON. Columbia's Legacy; or, WASHINGTON'S Valuable Advice to his Fellow Citizens, published by him at the period of announcing his intention of retiring from Public Life at the expiration of the present Constitutional Term of the Presidency of the United States. To which is added, his *Speech* to *Congress*, at their present session, which terminates his political career. *Portrait of Washington inserted.* 16*mo, pp.* 89, *Original Sheep binding.*

Philadelphia, December 10th, 1796

In fine preservation, and of great rarity.

571 WASHINGTON. Correspondence of the American Revolution; being Letters of Eminent Men to George Washington, from the time of his taking command of the Army to the end of his Presidency. 4 *vols. Imperial 8vo, cloth, uncut.*

LARGE PAPER. Boston, 1853

Portraits of Washington inserted in each volume to face title pages.

Fowle, tree calf $14.00, per vol. Bruce, half Russia, uncut, $10.50 per vol. Morrell, $2.00 per vol.

572 WASHINGTON. CORRY, JOHN. The Life of George Washington, late President, and Commander-in-Chief of the

United States of America; Interspersed with Biographical Anecdotes of the most Eminent Men who effected the American Revolution, etc. *Rare Portrait inserted. Small, 8vo, pp.* 228. *Full crimson levant morocco, crushed, gilt back, and rich inside borders, gilt top, uncut, by Bedford.* London, 1800

Superb copy and of excessive rarity in uncut condition.

573 WASHINXATON. CORRY, JOHN. Life of George Washington, late President and Commander-in-Chief of the Armies of the United States of America. New Edition. *Curious Portrait. Small* 8*vo, pp.* 57, *with Index,* 2 *pp. uncut. Fine copy, very rare.* London, 1802

574 WASHINGTON. DANA, DANIEL. Discourse on the Character and Virtues of General George Washington, etc. 8*vo, pp.* 31, *uncut.* Newburyport, 1800

574* Diary of Washington, from the first day of October, 1789, to the 10th day of March, 1790. From the *Original Manuscript,* now first printed. *Portrait, and Letter Signed by* WASHINGTON, *New York, July* 9, 1789, *to* BEVERLY RANDOLPH, *inserted. Royal* 8*vo, full crimson morocco, gilt edges.*

PRIVATELY PRINTED. *Only* 100 *copies.*

New York, 1858

This rare volume, edited by Mr. Benson J. Lossing, is one of the few copies privately printed by Mr. Carson Brevoort, having the title printed in black. Those issued by the Club, have rubricated titles.

Corner, half morocco, $21.00. Roche, uncut, $21.00.

575 WASHINGTON. DIARY OF WASHINGTON: from the first day of October, 1789, to the 10th day of March, 1790, from the *Original Manuscript,* with Introductory Remarks by B. J. Lossing. *Photograph from Mme. de Brienne's miniature, alluded to at page* 12 *of the Diary, inserted. Royal* 8*vo, full crimson morocco, extra, by Matthews.* New York, 1858

ONLY 100 COPIES PRINTED.

The above copy (No. 12), was presented to the Brooklyn and Long Island Sanitary Fair by J. Carson Brevoort, Esq., and has a long historical note, in the autograph of the donor, appended.

576 WASHINGTON. DIARY OF WASHINGTON: from the first day of October, 1789, to the 10th day of March, 1790. From the *Original Manuscript*, now first printed. *Royal 8vo, uncut.*

PRIVATELY PRINTED: *only* 100 *copies.*

New York, 1858

Rubricated Title. This rare volume, the second of the privately printed issues of "The Club," was edited by Mr. Benson J. Lossing. Wight, morocco, extra plates, $75. Allan, morocco, extra plates, $50. Morrell, half morocco, extra plates, $40. Whitman, morocco, $37. Roche, $25.

577 WASHINGTON. Diary of George Washington, from 1789 to 1791; embracing the opening of the First Congress, and his Tours through New England, Long Island, and the Southern States. Together with his Journal of a Tour to the Ohio, in 1753. Edited by Benson J. Lossing. 12*mo, sheets. Scarce in this condition.*

New York, 1860

Morrell, $3.50. Roche, $3.00.

578 WASHINGTON. Diary of George Washington, from 1789 to 1791; embracing the Opening of the First Congress, and his Tours through New England, Long Island, and the Southern States, Together with his Journal of a Tour to the Ohio, in 1753. Edited by Benson J. Lossing. *8vo, half morocco, gilt top, uncut, by Matthews.*

LARGE PAPER: *but few printed.*

Richmond: Press of the Historical Society, 1861

Inserted in this volume are THREE *fine portraits of Washington, after paintings by Gulligher, Savage, and Trumbull.*

579 WASHINGTON. DUNHAM, JOSIAH. Funeral Oration on George Washington, late General of the Armies of the

United States, etc. By Josiah Dunham, A. M. Capt. 16th U. S. Regiment. *8vo, pp.* 20. *Scarce.*

Boston, 1800

Presentation copy, with Autograph. Has curious Postscript.

580 WASHINGTON. EDMONDS, CYRUS R. Life and Times of General Washington. *Full length Portrait of Washington, and Plate of Washington's Triumphal Journey to the Capital, designed by* GEORGE CRUIKSHANK, *also Fac-similes.* 2 *vols.* 12*mo, boards, uncut.*

London, Tegg, 1835

The Portrait of Washington is a reduced one of Heath's celebrated engraving.

581 WASHINGTON. Eulogies and Orations on the Life and Death of *General George Washington,* First President of the United States of America. *8vo, sheep. Fine clean copy.* Boston, 1800

With list of subscribers.

Wight, $9.25.

582 WASHINGTON. EVERETT, EDWARD. Life of George Washington. *Portraits. Beautiful Bank-Note Vignette portrait inserted in Title page.* 8*vo, cloth, uncut.*

LARGE PAPER: 100 COPIES PRINTED.

New York, 1860

Finely printed in large type on heavy plate paper.

Morrell, $5.00. Whitmore, $3.00. Roche, $3.00.

Mr. Wight's copy, extended to quarto size, morocco, 135 extra plates, $180.

583 WASHINGTON. LETTERS OF THE TWO COMMANDERS-IN-CHIEF, GENERALS GAGE AND WASHINGTON, and Major-Generals BURGOYNE and LEE; with the *Manifesto* of GENERAL WASHINGTON to the *Inhabitants of Canada, pp.* 8. New York, James Rivington, 1775

PRESENT POLITICAL STATE OF THE PROVINCE OF MASSA-

CHUSETTS BAY in General, and the Town of BOSTON in Particular, etc. *By a Native of New England, pp.* 86.
New York, Rivington, 1775

PATRIOTS OF NORTH AMERICA: a Sketch with Explanatory Notes, *pp.* 47. New York, 1775

AMERICANS ROUSED IN A CURE FOR THE SPLEEN, etc., *pp.* 32. New York, Rivington, n. d.

ALARM TO THE LEGISLATURE OF THE PROVINCE OF NEW YORK, occasioned by the present Political Disturbances, etc., *pp.* 13. New York, Rivington, 1775

WHAT THINK YE OF CONGRESS NOW? etc., *pp.* 48
New York, Rivington, 1775

POOR MAN'S ADVICE TO HIS NEIGHBOURS: A *Ballad* to the Tune of Chevy Chase, *pp.* 19. New York, 1774

FRIENDLY ADDRESS TO ALL REASONABLE AMERICANS, etc. *pp.* 55. New York, 1774

With other scarce Pamphlets, in all 24, *nearly all printed by* JAMES RIVINGTON *the Tory Printer of the Revolution. Excessively rare. Thick* 8*vo, green morocco.*
New York, etc., 1774, 1775

584 WASHINGTON. LETTERS WRITTEN BY GENERAL WASHINGTON TO HENRY LAURENS, President of the Continental Congress. 9000

1. Valley Forge, January 31, 1778, 3 *pp. folio.*
2. " " April 30, 1778, 4 *pp. folio,* (*stained.*)
3. " " May 29, 1778, 3 *pp. folio.*
4. Headquarters, August 20, 1778, 4 *pp. folio.*

Portrait of Washington. Proof before Letters, engraved by Hall, from an Original Miniature by Wm. Birch, in the possession of Charles G. Barney, Esq. Private Plate. Title page beautifully drawn, and illuminated by hand in gold and colors.

Folio, full rich green morocco, extra, inside borders of gold.

New York, 1867

The intense historical interest associated with the above ORIGINAL AUTOGRAPH LETTERS *of* WASHINGTON, *cannot be overestimated; the first, written at Valley Forge, January,* 31, 1778, *to* HENRY LAURENS, *President of Congress, respecting the cabal which existed against him in Congress and in the Army, and vindicating himself against the aspersions of General Conway and others, is here given in full.*

GEORGE WASHINGTON TO HENRY LAURENS, Valley Forge, 31 January, 1778:—SIR; I this morning received your favor of the 27th instant. I cannot sufficiently express the obligation I feel to you, for your friendship and politeness upon all occasions in which I am so deeply interested. I was not unapprized that a malignant faction had been for some time formiug to my prejudice: which, conscious as I am of having ever done all in my power to answer the important purposes of the trust reposed in me, could not but give me some pain on a personal account. But my chief concern arises from an apprehension of the dangerous consequences, which intestine dissensions may produce to the common cause.

As I have no other view than to promote the public good, and am unambitious of honors not founded in the approbation of my country, I would not desire in the last degree to suppress a free spirit of inquiry into any part of my conduct, that even a faction itself may deem reprehensible. The anonymous paper handed to you exhibits many serious charges, and it is my wish that it should be submitted to Congress. This I am the more inclined to, as the suppression or concealment, may possibly involve you in embarrassments hereafter, since it is uncertain how many or who may be privy to the contents.

My enemies take an ungenerous advantage of me. They know the delicacy of my situation, and that motives of policy deprive me of the defence I might otherwise make against their insidious attacks. They know I cannot combat their insinuations, however injurious, without disclosing secrets which is of the utmost moment to conceal. But why should I expect to be exempt from censure, the unfailing lot of an elevated station? Merit and talents, with which I can have no pretensions of rivalship, have ever been subject to it. My heart tells me that it has been my uuremitted aim to do the best that circumstances would permit; yet I may have been very often mistaken in my judgment of thc means, and may in many instances deserve the imputation of error. I cannot forbear repeating, that I have a grateful sense of the favorable disposition you have manifested to me in this affair, and beg you will believe me to be, with sentiments of real esteem and regard, Sir,

Your much obliged and obed't servant,

GEORGE WASHINGTON.

The Hon'ble HENRY LAURENS, ESQ., Pres't Congress.

585 WASHINGTON. PEALE. Catalogue of Valuable Original Paintings by the Late REMBRANDT PEALE, with Engrav-

ings, etc., comprising the contents of the Studio of this Eminent Artist. To be sold without reserve, November 18th, 1862, etc. *Fine Autograph Letter of Peale, 1 p. 4to, Boston, June 20, 1828, also Portrait of Washington, after Painting by Peale, inserted.* 8vo, *half morocco, gilt top, by Matthews.* Philadelphia, 1862

Contains interesting account of the Portraits of Washington, painted by Peale, with the Testimonials in reference, from Chief-Justice Marshall, Judge Washington, Judge Peters, Charles Carroll, Bishop White, Col. Tallmadge, and others.

586 WASHINGTON. Fac-similes of Letters from his Excellency George Washington, President of the United States of America, to Sir John Sinclair, Bart., M. P., on Agricultural and other Interesting Topics, etc. *Portrait and Views of Mt. Vernon and Washington's Tomb. Autograph Letter (Edinburgh,* 1831), *of Sir John Sinclair, inserted, also fine Portrait engraved by Bromley.* Washington, 1844

587 WASHINGTON. FAREWELL ADDRESS. George Washington to the People of the United States, Announcing his Intention of Retiring from Public Life. *Fine Portrait engraved by Edwin. Royal* 8vo, *crimson morocco, gilt. Original binding.*
Very rare. Philadelphia, 1800

Newspaper cuttings inserted.
Whiteman, $15.00.

588 WASHINGTON. Farewell Address to the People of the United States. *Portrait,* 12*mo, half morocco, gilt.* New Brunswick, 1812

589 WASHINGTON. Farewell Address to the People of the United States. *View of Mount Vernon, etc., with Ornamental Title page, and Arabesque designs.* 4*to, uncut.* Philadelphia, 1858

590 WASHINGTON. JOHN FITCH. Sermon delivered at Dan-

ville at the Request of Harmony Lodge; as a Tribute of Respect for the Memory of the Late General George Washington, February 26th, 1800. *8vo, pp.* 24, *uncut. Scarce.* Peacham, Vermont, 1800

591 WASHINGTON. FLINT, ABEL. Discourse delivered at Hartford February 22, 1800, the Day set apart by recommendation of Congress, to pay a Tribute of Respect to the Memory of General George Washington, who died December 14th 1799. *8vo, pp.* 22 Hartford, 1800

592 WASHINGTON. FOX, CHARLES. A Portrait of George Washington, from an Original Drawing, as he appeared while reviewing the Continental Army on Boston Common, in 1776. A History of the Portrait, and Documentary Evidence in proof of the correctness of the likeness. *Portrait. Royal 8vo, cloth.* Boston, 1851

Morrell, $3.00. Fisher, $2.25.

593 WASHINGTON. GUIZOT. Washington. Translated by Henry Reeve, Esq. *Portrait inserted. Crown 8vo, cloth, uncut.* London, Murray, 1840

Fine, large type edition of Guizot's beautiful Essay on the Life and Character of Washington.

594 WASHINGTON. [The Same.] Washington. *In French. Post 8vo, Russia, gilt.* London, 1841

595 WASHINGTON. HOLCOMBE, HENRY. A Sermon occasioned by the Death of Lieutenant-General George Washington, late President of the United States of America, etc. By Henry Holcombe, *Minister of the Word of God in Savannah. Small 4to, pp.* 18, *uncut. Very Scarce.* Savannah, 1800

Morrell, $5.00. Roche, $4.50. H. A. Smith, $3.75.

596 WASHINGTON. [The Same.] *Small 4to, pp.* 18, *uncut.* Savannah, 1800

597 WASHINGTON. HOUDIN'S LAST RESPECTS TO GEORGE WASHINGTON. *Very rare Portrait of Washington inserted, also Autograph Letter of Michael G. Houdin* (3 *pp* 4*to*, *Albany*, *October* 22, 1800.) 8*vo*, *pp*. 7. *Morocco extra*, *gilt back and edges*, *by Matthews.*
Albany, 1800

The Compiler cannot learn of another copy of this excessively rare pamphlet.

598 WASHINGTON. IRVING, WASHINGTON. Life of George Washington. *Numerous fine Plates, many on India paper, after Paintings by F. O. C. Darley, and others.* 5 *vols.* 4*to*, *cloth*, *uncut*.
LARGE PAPER: 100 *copies only printed.*
New York, 1855–59

THIS COPY IS ONE OF A VERY FEW HAVING THE ORIGINAL AUTOGRAPH OF THE AUTHOR ON THE REVERSE OF TITLE PAGE, "WASHINGTON IRVING, NEW YORK, APRIL 9, 1856."

Fowle, $19.00 per vol. Fisher, $14.50 per vol. Roche, $13.00 per vol. Whitman, $13.00 per vol.

Morrell, extended to 10 vols. morocco, 1100 inserted Plates, etc., $200 per vol.

Wight, extended to 10 vols., unbound, 1036 Plates, etc., inserted, $77.50 per vol.

Allan, extended to 5 vols., half morocco, inserted Plates, etc., $55.00 per vol.

599 WASHINGTON. [The Same.] *Fine steel Plates, the same as in the quarto edition. Royal* 8*vo*, *uncut*, *in* 68 *numbers*, *as originally issued.*
PUBLISHED BY SUBSCRIPTION. New York, 1857–59

600 WASHINGTON. Journal of Major George Washington, sent by the Hon. Robert Dinwiddie, Esq., His Majesty's Lieutenant-Governor and Commander-in-Chief of Virginia, to the Commandant of the French Forces on *Ohio*. To which are added, the Governor's Letter; and a Translation of the *French* Officer's Answer, with a new Map of the Country as far as the *Mississippi*. *Map.* 8*vo*, *pp*. 32, *green levant morocco extra*, *gilt*

edges, with deep inside borders, richly tooled. Excessively rare. Williamsburg, Printed; London, Reprinted, 1754

Rare Portrait of Washington inserted, also Autograph. ("Head-quarters. Morristown, Jan. 12, 1777, George Washington.")
This copy, the only one sold at Auction in this city in many years, formerly belonged to the present owner, and brought at his sale in 1866, $46.00. *Was repurchased at Mr. Roche's sale in* 1867 *for* $49.00.

1 00 | 601 WASHINGTON. [The Same.] *Map. Royal* 8*vo, uncut.* LARGE PAPER: 50 *copies printed. Williamsburgh* (1754), *London, Reprinted* 1754, *New York, Reprinted* 1865

75 | 602 WASHINGTON. KIRKLAND, MRS. C. M. Memoirs of Washington. *Portrait and Plates.* 12*mo, cloth.* New York, 1857

2 50 | 603 WASHINGTON. Last Will and Testament of Gen. George Washington. 12*mo, uncut. Scarce.* Boston, Feb., 1800

50 | 604 WASHINGTON. LEE, Major-General HENRY. Funeral Oration on the Death of General Washington. Delivered at the request of Congress. 8*vo, pp.* 15. Boston, 1800

605 WASHINGTON. [The Same.] 8*vo, pp.* 17. Philadelphia, 1800

1 00 | 606 WASHINGTON. LEE, Major-General HENRY, and MINOT, Judge. Funeral Oration on the Death of George Washington, etc., delivered at the Request of Congress, by Major-General Henry Lee. To which is subjoined, An Eulogy; by Judge Minot. 8*vo. pp.* 28, *uncut.* London, 1800

Morrell, $4.50. Roche, $4.00.

50 | 607 WASHINGTON. [The Same.] 8*vo, pp.* 28, *uncut.* London, 1800

25 | 608 WASHINGTON. Letter to the People of the United States of

America, from *General Washington*, on his *Resignation* of the Office of President of the United States. 8*vo*, *pp*. 32. London, 1796

609 WASHINGTON. Letters from his Excellency General Washington, to Arthur Young, Esq., F R. S. Containing, an Account of his Husbandry, with a Map of his Farm etc. *Map*, 8*vo*, *pp*. 172, *uncut*. London, 1801

610 WASHINGTON. Life of General George Washington, late President of the United States of America, and Commander in Chief of their Armies, during the Revolutionary War. Dedicated to the Youth of America. 12*mo*, *pp*. 143. *Full smooth calf, gilt back, by Bedford. Rare.* Poughkeepsie, 1812

611 WASHINGTON. Life of General George Washington, late President of the United States of America, and Commander in Chief of their Armies, during the Revolutionary War. Dedicated to the Youth of America. 12*mo*, *pp*. 144. *Full polished calf, gilt back, by Bedford, Rare.* Boston, 1815

612 WASHINGTON. LOSSING, BENSON J. Life of Washington; A Biography, Personal, Military and Political. *Numerous fine steel plates.* 3 *vols*, *Roy*. 8*vo*, *half morocco*. New York, 1859

613 WASHINGTON. LOSSING, BENSON J. The Home of Washington and its Associations, Historical, Biographical and Pictorial. New Edition, Revised, with Additions. Illustrated by numerous Engravings, chiefly from original Drawings by the Author, engraved by Lossing and Barritt. *Fine impressions of the wood-cuts, Portrait of Washington, and newspaper cuttings inserted. Roy.* 8*vo*, *cloth*, *uncut*.
LARGE PAPER: 100 *Copies printed.* New York, 1865

Morrell, $12.50. Roche, $8.50.

614 WASHINGTON. MARSH, EBENEZER GRANT. An Oration delivered at Wethersfield, February 22, 1800; on the Death of General George Washington, etc. *8vo, pp.* 16. Hartford, 1800

H. A. Smith, $4.00.

615 WASHINGTON. MARSHALL, JOHN. Life of George Washington, Commander in Chief of the American Forces, during the war which established the Independence of his Country, etc. *Portrait, Views and Maps.* *5 vols, 8vo, half calf. Fine copy.* London, 1804

616 WASHINGTON. Memory of Washington: comprising a sketch of his Life and Character, and the National Testimonials of Respect. Also, a collection of Eulogies and Orations, with a copious index. *Rare and curious Portrait of Washington. 12mo, full levant morocco, by Matthews. Beautiful copy. Very scarce.* Newport, R. I., 1800

Allan, sheep, Portrait, wanting, $10. Morrell, sheep, Portrait wanting, $9.50

617 WASHINGTON. MINOT, GEORGE RICHARDS. An Eulogy on George Washington, late Commander in Chief of the Armies of the United States of America, who died December 14, 1799, etc. Second Edition. *8vo, pp.* 24, *uncut.* Boston, 1800

Morrell, $7.00.

618 WASHINGTON. [The Same.] *8vo, pp.* 24, *uncut.* Boston, 1800

619 WASHINGTON. M'GUIRE, E. C. Religious Opinions and Character of Washingtou. *12mo, cloth.* New York, 1836

620 WASHINGTON. Minutes of a Conspiracy against the Liberties of America. *Fine Portrait on India paper, of*

Washington after Stuart's picture inserted. Folio, uncut.

LARGE PAPER: 25 *copies printed.*

Philadelphia, 1865

Originally printed in 1786. *Contains an Account of the celebrated "Hickey Plot," in which an attempt was made to assassinate General Washington.*

621 WASHINGTON. Monuments of Washington's Patriotism; containing a Fac-simile of his Publick Accounts kept during the Revolutionary War; and some of the most interesting Documents connected with his Military Command and Civil Administration, etc. Together with an Eulogium on the Character of Washington, by Major W. Jackson, one of his Aids-de-Camp. *Portrait and Fac-similes of Continental Money. Folio, cloth.* City of Washington, 1838

Morrell, $6.50.

622 WASHINGTON. Monuments of Washington's Patriotism; containing a Fac-simile of his Publick Accounts kept during the Revolutionary War; and some of the most interesting Documents connected with his Military Command and Civil Administration, etc. *Portraits, Views of Mt. Vernon and Washington's Sarcophagus. Folio, morocco, gilt.* Washington, 1841

Wight, $4.50.

623 WASHINGTON. MORSE, JEDIDIAH. Sermon delivered at *Charlestown*, in the Commonwealth of Massachusetts, February 19, 1795; being the Day recommended by *George Washington*, President of the United States of America, for *Public Thanksgiving and Prayer. 8vo. pp.* 37, *uncut.* Boston, 1795

624 WASHINGTON. MORSE, JEDIDIAH. A Prayer and Sermon delivered at Charlestown, December 31, 1799, on the death of George Washington, late President and Com-

mander-in-Chief of the Armies of the United States of America, etc. With an Additional Sketch of his Life, etc., etc. *8vo, pp.* 44, 36, *uncut.* London, 1800

Wight, $3.75

625 Washington. Native American. A Gift for the People. Containing Washington's Farewell Address, Declaration of Independence, Constitution of the United States, etc. *Portraits of Washington, Franklin, Adams and Jefferson. Royal* 8vo, *half morocco.* Philadelphia, 1845

This volume is "appropriately printed with *red* ink, in *blue* borders, on *white* paper."

626 Washington. Official Letters to the Honourable American Congress, written during the War between the United Colonies and Great Britain, by his Excellency George Washington, Commander-in-Chief of the Continental Forces, now President of the United States. *Rare Portrait after Savage, engraved by Hill, fine impression.* 2 *vols.* 12*mo, sheep.* Boston, 1796

Copies containing the Portrait are seldom met with.

627 Washington. Paine, Thomas. An Eulogy on the Life of General George Washington, who died at Mount Vernon, December 14th, 1799, in the 68th year of his age, etc. *8vo, pp.* 22, *uncut.* Newburyport, 1800

Morrell, $6.75.

628 Washington. [The Same.] *8vo. uncut.* Newburyport, 1800

629 Washington. Pictorial Life of George Washington: embracing Anecdotes illustrative of his Character. *Colored Plates. Square* 12*mo, cloth.* Philadelphia, 1847

630 Washington. Poetical Epistle to his Excellency, George Washington, Esq., Commander-in-Chief of the Armies

of the United States of America, from an Inhabitant of the State of Maryland. To which is annexed A SHORT SKETCH of General WASHINGTON'S Life and Character. 5 *Portraits of Washington inserted. Small 4to, half morocco.*

50 COPIES ONLY REPRINTED. Annapolis, Printed, 1779 London, Reprinted, 1780. New York, Reprinted, 1865

Fisher, $3.25.
A copy of the London Reprint, 1780, *morocco extra, by Matthews sold in Morrell's sale for* $46.00.

631 WASHINGTON. PORTRAITS, A COLLECTION OF 85 ENGRAVED PORTRAITS OF WASHINGTON, all different, many being of excessive rarity; proofs on India paper, etc., neatly mounted in Scrap Book. *Imperial 4to, half crimson levant morocco, gilt edges.*

The above were collected with a view to inserting in "Tuckerman's Essay on the Portraits of Washington, and consist of engravings by Savage, Rollinson, Fittler, Tanner, Nutter, Leney, Durand, Prudhomme, Gimbrede, Kelly, Furman, etc., etc., after paintings by Stuart, Trumbull, Alex Campbell, Savage, J. Peale, Woolley, Dunlap, Robertson, C. W. Beale, Bartoli, Chapman, etc.

632 WASHINGTON. RAMSAY, DAVID. Oration on the Death of Lieutenant General Washington, late President of the United States, who died Dec. 14, 1799, etc. *8vo, pp.* 30. Charleston, 1800

Wight, $4.00.

633 WASHINGTON. RAMSAY, DAVID. Life of George Washington, Commander in Chief of the Armies of the United States, in the war which established their Independence; and First President of the United States. *Fine Portrait engraved by Heath. 8vo, half green morocco, gilt top, uncut, rough edges. Fine copy,* London, 1807

634 WASHINGTON. RAMSAY, DAVID. Vie de Georges Washington, Genéral en Chef des Armées des Etats Unis,

etc. Traduit de L'Anglais. *Fine Portrait.* 8vo, *calf, gilt.* Paris, 1809

635 Washington. Ramsay, David. Life of George Washington, Commander in Chief of the Armies of the United States of America, throughout the war which established their Independence, etc. *Portrait.* 12mo, *sheep.* Boston, 1811

636 Washington, Remarks Occasioned by the Late Conduct of *Mr. Washington*, as President of the United States, M.DCC.XCVI. 8*vo, uncut.* Philadelphia, 1797

Fisher, half mor., $5.25. Morrell, half mor., uncut, $5.00.

637 Washington. Revolutionary Orders of General Washington, issued during the years 1778, '80, '81 and '82; selected from the MSS. of John Whiting, etc., and edited by his son, Henry Whiting, Lieut. Col. U. S. Army. *Portrait inserted.* 8*vo, half morocco, gilt top.* New York, 1844

Bruce, $3.00.

638 Washington. Selections of the *Patriotic Addresses* to the President of the United States, together with the President's *Answers*, etc. 12*mo, sheep.* Boston, 1798

639 Washington. Selections from the Correspondence of George Washington, and *James Anderson, LL.D.*, etc. 8*vo, pp.* 79, *uncut.* Charlestown, 1800

640 Washington. Simpkinson, John Nassau. The Washingtons, a Tale of a Country Parish in the Seventeenth Century. Based on Authentic Documents. *Plates. Crown* 8*vo, cloth, uncut. Scarce.* London, 1860

Contains a valuable historical account of the Ancestors of Washington. Dr. Stiles' copy sold in 1866, for $9.

Stiles, $9.00. Morrell, calf $5.00.

641 Washington. Smith, Jeremiah. Oration on the Death

of George Washington; delivered at Exeter, February 22, 1800. *8vo, pp. 31, uncut. Scarce.* Exeter, 1800

642 WASHINGTON. SNOWDEN, JAMES ROSS. Medallic Memorials of Washington in the Mint of the United States. 79 *Beautiful Engravings from Medals. Imperial 8vo, cloth.* Philadelphia, 1861 2 50

643 WASHINGTON. SPARKS, JARED. Life of George Washington, Commander-in-Chief of the American Armies, and First President of the United States, to which are added his Diaries and Speeches, and various Miscellaneous Papers relating to his Habits and Opinions. *Portraits on India paper. 2 vols. 8vo, cloth, uncut. Fine large type edition.* London, 1839 3 00

Portrait and Autograph Letter of JARED SPARKS *inserted, also several Portraits of* WASHINGTON, *etc.*
Morrell, $6.00 per vol.

644 WASHINGTON. SPARKS, JARED. Life of George Washington. *Plates, including the beautiful Portrait of Washington engraved by A. B. Durand after Stuart's Painting. 8vo, cloth, uncut. Early Edition.* Boston, 1844 2 00

645 WASHINGTON. STEARNS, ELISHA. Eulogium on General George Washington; Spoken at Tolland, on the 22nd of February, 1800, at the request of the Inhabitants. 12*mo, pp. 24, uncut. Very rare.* East Windsor, July, 29, 1800 6 50

646 WASHINGTON. STORY, ISAAC. Eulogy on the Glorious Virtues of the Illustrious General George Washington, who died at *Mount Vernon*, December 14, 1799, in the 68th year of his age—*ripe in honor and full of glory. 8vo, pp. 23, uncut.* Worcester, 1800 5 00

647 WASHINGTON. STORY, NATHAN. Discourse delivered on Friday, December 27, 1799, the Day set apart by the 3 50

Citizens of Hartford, to lament before God, the Death of General George Washington, etc. *8vo, pp.* 31. Hartford, 1800

648 WASHINGTON. TRUMBULL, BENJAMIN. Funeral Discourse delivered at North Haven, December 29, 1799, on the death of General George Washington, etc. *Rare Portrait, engraved by Doolittle. 8vo, pp.* 31, *half morocco. Scarce.* New Haven, 1800

Roche, uncut, $6.00.

649 WASHINGTON. TUCKERMAN, HENRY T. The Character and Portraits of Washington. *Portraits on India Paper. Portrait of Tuckerman, and Newspaper cutting relative to Portraits of Washington inserted.* 4*to, uncut, in portfolio. Very scarce.* New York, 1859

ONLY 156 COPIES PRINTED.
Morrell, $20. Whiteman, $16. Bruce, 12.50.

650 WASHINGTON. TUCKERMAN, JOSEPH. Funeral Oration occasioned by the death of General George Washington, written at the request of the *Boston Mechanic's Association, etc.* 8*vo, pp.* 24. Boston, 1800

651 WASHINGTON. UPHAM, REV. C. W. Life of Gen. Washington, First President of the United States, written by himself; comprising his Memoirs and Correspondence, etc. *Portraits of Washington and Franklin, and views of the "Seige of New York," and "Surrender at Saratoga."* 2 *vols, crown* 8*vo, cloth, uncut.* London, 1852

Wight, half Russia, $2.00 per vol. Roche, half Russia, uncut, $2.00 per vol.

652 WASHINGTON. UPHAM, CHARLES W. [The Same.] *Portrait inserted.* 2 *vols,* 12*mo, half calf, gilt.* Boston, 1840

653 WASHINGTON. Washingtoniana; containing a sketch of the

Life and Death of the late General George Washington; with a collection of elegant Eulogies, Orations, Poems, etc., sacred to his Memory; also, an appendix comprising all his most Valuable Public Papers, and his last Will and Testament. *Portrait, engraved by Edwin. 8vo, sheep. Fine copy.* Lancaster, 1802

Morrell, $10. Wight, $9.50. Whiteman, $8,50. Corner, $7.50. Smith, $7.00. Whitmore, $5.75.

654 WASHINGTON. Washingtoniana; or Memorials of the Death of George Washington, giving an Account of the Funeral Honors paid to his Memory, with a List of Tracts and Volumes printed upon the occasion, and a Catalogue of Medals commemorating the Event. By Franklin B. Hough. *Portraits on India paper, and Map. 2 vols, 4to, uncut.* 2 25

LARGE PAPER: *only* 85 *copies printed.*

W. Elliot Woodward, Roxbury, Mass., 1865

Morrell, $6.75 per vol. Cornor, $5.50 per vol. Bruce, $5,00 per vol.

655 WASHINGTON. Washington Chair, presented to the New York Historical Society, by Benjamin Robert Winthrop, 1857. *Plates. 8vo, cloth.* New York, 1857 1 75

EDITION LIMITED.
Whitmore, $1.50. Roche, $1.50.

656 WASHINGTON. WEEMS, REV. M. L. A History of the Life and Death, Virtues and Exploits, of *Gen. George Washington*, Faithfully taken from Authentic Documents, and now, in a Second Edition Improved; Respectfully offered to the perusal of his Countrymen; as also, all others who wish to see Human Nature in its most finished form. *Rare Portrait of Washington. 8vo, green crushed levant morocco, gilt, with rich inside borders, by Matthews.* Philadelphia, 1800 12 00

The octavo edition of this well known biography is of great rarity. Inserted in this copy is a beautiful woodcut Portrait on tinted paper of the Author, Dr. Weems.

657 WASHINGTON. WEEMS, REV. M. L. Life of George Washington, with Curious Anecdotes, equally honourable to himself, and exemplary to his young Countrymen. *Portrait and Map, with curious engravings of Braddock's Defeat, the Battle of Lexington, etc. 12mo, half morocco, gilt back and edges.* Philadelphia, 1818

658 WASHINGTON. WEEMS, REV. M. L. Life of George Washington, With Curious Anecdotes, equally honourable to himself, and exemplary to his young Countrymen. Twenty-sixth Edition greatly improved. *Portrait, Map, and Plates, comprising curious representations of the Battle of Lexington, Capture of André, etc., etc.* 12*mo, sheep.* Philadelphia, 1824

659 WASHINGTON. WETMORE, REV. ROBERT G. Oration occasioned by the Death of Lieutenant-General George Washington. Delivered at the Lutheran Church, in Scoharie, on the 15th of January, 1800. To which is added the Order of Procession, and a number of elegiac Odes. 12*mo, pp.* 20, *uncut.* Cooperstown, 1800

One of the rarest of Washington Eulogies. Probably imperfect, as the ODES *are wanting, though they may never have been printed. Not knowing of another copy, it has been impossible to compare by collating.*

660 WASHINGTON. Writings of George Washington; being his Correspondence Addresses, Messages, and other Papers, Official and Private, Selected and Published from the Original Manuscripts; with a Life of the Author, Notes and Illustrations, by Jared Sparks. *Portraits, Maps, etc.* 12 *vols. Imperial* 8*vo, boards, uncut.* LARGE PAPER: *Fine, clean copy.* Boston, 1834

Name of previous owner has been cut from Title pages of volumes 2 *and* 3, *otherwise a splendid copy.*

Fowle, tree calf, $25 per vol. Bruce, half Russia uncut, $10.50 per vol. Whitmore, $8.00 per vol. Whiteman, $6.75 per vol. Wight, $6.00 per vol. Roche, $5.75 per vol.

661 WATSON, ELKANAH. History of the Rise, Progress and

Existing Condition of the *Western Canals* in the State of New York, from September, 1788, to the completion of the Middle Section of the *Grand Canal*, in 1812, etc. *Fine Portrait of Elkanah Watson, and Maps.* 8*vo, calf, gilt.* Albany, 1820

Morrell, boards, uncut, $3.00.

662 WAYNE. Orderly Book of the Northern Army, at Ticonderoga and Mt. Independence, from October 17th, 1776, to January 8th, 1777, with Biographical and Explanatory Notes, and an Appendix. *Portrait and Map.* 4*to, uncut.* Albany, 1859
LARGE PAPER: *only* 10 *copies printed.*
Munsell's Historical Series, No. 3.

663 WEBSTER, NOAH. Collections of Essays and Fugitive Writings, on Moral, Historical, Political and Literary Subjects. *Portrait inserted.* 8*vo, sheep,* Boston, 1790

Contains "Sketches of the American Revolution." "Remarks on Indian Funerals, etc."

664 WELD, JUN., ISAAC. Travels through the States of North America, and the Provinces of Upper and Lower Canada, during the years 1795, 1796 and 1797. 16 *Fine Plates, including views of Mt. Vernon, Natural Bridge, etc.* 2 *vols. in* 1. 8*vo, half crimson morocco, uncut.* London, Stockdale, 1807

665 WELDE, T. A Short Story of the Rise, Reign and Ruin of the *Antinomians, Familists* and *Libertines* that infected the *Churches of* NEW ENGLAND; and how they were Confuted by the Assembly of Ministers there. As also of the Magistrate's Proceedings in Court against them. Together with God's Strange, Remarkable Judgements from Heaven upon some of the Chief Fomenters of these Opinions; and the lamentable death of *Mrs. Hutchinson*, etc. *Small* 4*to. pp.* 64. *Full*

crimson levant morocco, gilt back, inside borders and edges, by Pratt. London, 1692

Beautiful clean copy, with large margins of this very rare tract.
Morrell, Title inlaid, calf, $26.

666 WESTERN ANNALS. Annals of the West; embracing a Concise Account of *Principal Events* which have occurred in the *Western States* and *Territories* from the Discovery of the *Mississippi Valley* to the year eighteen hundred and fifty-six. Compiled from the most Authentic Sources, and published by James L. Albach. *Thick royal 8vo, pp.* 1016, *sheep.* Pittsburgh, 1857

667 WESTERN WORLD. The United States. *Fine steel plate Vignette engraved by Finden, representing "Washington taking leave of his Officers," etc.* 2 *vols. post 8vo, boards, uncut.* London, 1830–32

668 WETMORE, PROSPER M. Lexington, with other Fugitive Poems. *Portraits of General Wetmore, Clara Fisher, and other plates inserted.* 8vo, *boards, uncut. Scarce.* New York, 1830

Morrell, extra plates, morocco, $21.00. Whitmore, no plates, $3.00. Whiteman, no plates, $3.00. Roche, no plates, $2.25.

669 WHEATLEY, PHILLIS. Poems on Various Subjects, Religious and Moral. By Phillis Wheatley, NEGRO SERVANT TO MR. JOHN WHEATLEY, OF BOSTON IN NEW ENGLAND. *Curious Portrait, fine impression. Small 8vo, original sheep binding. Rare.* London, 1773

Fisher, half morocco, uncut, $15.

670 WHITBOURNE, RICHARD. A Discovrse and Discovery of NEW-FOVND LAND, With many reasons to proove how worthy and *beneficiall a Plantation may there be made,* after a better manner than it was. Together with a laying open of certaine Enormities and abuses commit-

ted by some that trade to that *Countrey, and the meanes laid downe for reformation thereof. Written by Captaine Richard Whitbourne, etc.* As also a louing Institution: and likewise the copies of certaine Letters sent from that Countrey, which are printed in *the latter part of this Booke. Royal Arms on reverse of Title. Small 4to, full polished calf, by Bedford. Very rare.* London, 1623

671 WHITE, GEORGE. Statistics of the State of Georgia; including an Account of its Natural, Civil, and Ecclesiastical History, etc., with Notices of the Manners and Customs of its Aboriginal Tribes. *Map. Thick 8vo, cloth.* Savannah, 1849

Wight. $2.88.

672 WHITE, STEPHEN. Sermon occasioned by the lamentable death of *Col.* JOSEPH TRUMBULL, ESQ., who departed this life, July 23d, 1778, and delivered in the First Society in Lebanon, at his *Interment,* July the 24th. *8vo, pp. 17, uncut. Very scarce.* Hartford, 1779

673 WHITEFIELD, GEORGE. Journal of a Voyage from London to Savannah, in Georgia, with continuation, etc. *Post 8vo, cloth.* London, 1830

674 WHITEHEAD, WILLIAM A. Contributions to the Early History of Perth Amboy and adjoining County, with sketches of Men and Events in New Jersey, during the Provincial Era. *Maps and Engravings, including portraits of Governor Franklin, John Watson, early American Painter, etc. 8vo, cloth.* New York, 1856

675 WHITTIER, JOHN G. Poems, illustrated by H. Billings. *Fine Portrait, and illustrations on steel. 8vo, cloth, gilt.* Boston, 1849

676 WILKES, CHARLES. Narrative of the United States Ex-

ploring Expedition, during the years, 1838, 1839, 1840, 1841, 1842. *Portrait and numerous fine steelplates and woodcuts. Autograph, and* 2 *extra portraits of Commodore Wilkes inserted.* 5 *vols., with Atlas together;* 6 *vols., Roy.* 8*vo, cloth, uncut.* Philadelphia, 1845

677 WILKINSON, ELIZA. Letters, during the Invasion and Possession of Charleston, S. C., by the British in Revolutionary War. Arranged from the Original Manuscripts, by Caroline Gilman. 12*mo, cloth.* New York, 1839

Wight, $2.38. Morrell, half morocco, $2.00.

678 WILLARD, SAMUEL. A Complete BODY OF DIVINITY IN TWO HUNDRED AND FIFTY Expository Lectures on the Assembly's Shorter Catechism, wherein the Doctrines of the *Christian Religion* are unfolded, etc., etc. By the Reverend and Learned SAMUEL WILLARD, M. A., Late Pastor of the *South Church* in *Boston*, and Vice-President of *Harvard College in Cambridge, in New England. Folio, pp.* 914, *half brown morocco, red edges.* Boston, 1726

Portrait wanting.

679 WILLETS, MARINUS. Narrative of the Military Actions of Colonel Marinus Willett, taken Chiefly from his Own Manuscript. Prepared by his Son, William M. Willett. *Fine proof Portrait of Col. Willett.* 8*vo, boards, uncut, rough edges. Very rare.* New York, 1831

Fine clean copy, with original Historical Document, dated Fort Stanwix, 9th August, 1777, signed by SIR JOHN JOHNSON (*one of the rarest of American Autographs*), *inserted; also, View of Major Willett's residence, and cuttings.*
Roche, no extra matter, $10.

680 WILLIAMS, REV. ELEAZER. Life of Te-ho-ra-gwa-ne-gen, alias *Thomas Williams*, a Chief of the Caughnawaga

Tribe of Indians in Canada. *Rare original receipt to United States Store-Keeper, Detroit, July* 25, 1820, *for Ordinance Stores for " the use of a party of the Six-Nations of Indians," signed,* " ELEAZER WILLIAMS," *inserted. Royal* 8*vo, cloth.* Albany, Munsell, 1859
ONLY 200 COPIES PRINTED.

Whiteman, morocco, $5.50. Wight, half morocco, $4.00. Roche, half morocco, $4.00.

681 WILLIAMS. STEPHEN W. American Medical Biography; or, Memoirs of Eminent Physicians, etc. *Portraits.* 8*vo, cloth.* Greenfield, Mass., 1859 8 00

Intended as a Supplement to DR. THACHER'S MEDICAL BIOGRAPHY. *See* THACHER.

682 WILSON. Orderly Book. Expedition of the British and Provincial Army, under Maj. Gen. Jeffrey Amherst, against Ticonderoga and Crown Point, 1759. *Map. Small* 4*to, boards, uncut.* Albany, 1857 5 00

Fowle, $60.

MUNSELL'S HISTORICAL SERIES, No. 1.

683 WIRT, WILLIAM. Letters of the British Spy. Originally published in the Virginia *Argus*, in August and September, 1803. Second Edition. *Two Portraits of Wirt and fine autograph letter, Washington, December* 4, 1820 *inserted.* 8*vo, boards. Scarce.* 3 75
Richmond, December, 1803

The *first* collected edition.

684 WOOD, SILAS. Sketch of the *First Settlement* of the several Towns on Long Island; with their Political Condition, to the end of the American Revolution. New Edition. *View of Battle Pass, Brooklyn, inserted.* 8*vo, boards. uncut. Rare.* Brooklyn, N. Y., 1828 9 00

Morrell, half morocco, uncut, $20. H. A. Smith, $8.25. Bruce, $5.

685 WOODWARD. HISTORICAL SERIES.

1, 2 *Records of Salem Witchcraft*, copied from the Original Documents, 1691–2. 2 *vols.*

200 COPIES PRINTED.

3, 4 *History of the Indian Wars in New England, etc.*, from the Original Work; by the Rev. William Hubbard, edited by Samuel G. Drake. *Map.* 2 *vols.*

300 COPIES PRINTED.

5, 6, 7 *Witchcraft Delusion in New England;* its Rise, Progress and Termination, as exhibited by Dr. Cotton Mather, and Mr. Robert Calef, etc. Edited by Samuel G. Drake. 3 *vols.*

280 COPIES PRINTED.

In all 7 *vols. Small* 4*to, uncut.*
Roxbury, Mass., 1864–1866

Volumes 1 *and* 2 *of this series have on several occasions brought from* $15 *to* $20 *each.*

686 WYNNE, JAMES Private Libraries of New York. 12 *plates inserted, consisting of fine Portraits of T. F. Dibdin, Isaac Walton, Samuel Rogers, John Allan, George Bancroft, Henry C. Murphy, W. E. Burton, etc., some being proofs on India paper. Thick Imperial* 8*vo, cloth, uncut.* New York, 1860

LARGE PAPER: 100 copies printed.

Fowle, morocco, $41. Morrell, plates inserted, half morocco, $37. H. A. Smith, half Russia, $21. Wight, half morocco, $18.50.

Contains view of the interior of the Library of William Curtis Noyes.

687 WYNNE, JAMES. [The Same.] *Plate, interior of W. C. Noyes' Library. Thick* 8*vo, crimson levant morocco, gilt top, uncut, by Matthews.* New York, 1860

EDITION LIMITED.

YOUNG, SAMUEL. A Wall Street Bear in Europe, with his Familiar Foreign Journal of a Tour through Portions of England, Scotland, France, and Italy. By T. Q. 12*mo, half crimson morocco, gilt top, uncut*

PRINTED FOR PRIVATE CIRCULATION. *Scarce.*

New York, 1855

Allan, extra plates, morocco, $11.50. Morrell, half morocco, $2.50.

689 YOUNG, ALEXANDER. Chronicles of the First Planters of the Colony of Massachusetts Bay, from 1623 to 1636. Now first collected from Original Records, etc., with Notes. *Portrait of Governor Winthrop.* 8vo, *cloth, uncut.*

Boston, 1846

Fowle, $3.50. Bruce, calf, $3.00. Whiteman, $2.75.

Addenda.

CAREW, BAMFYLDE MOORE. Life and Adventures of, the King of the Beggars, being an Account of his Life, etc., with his travels twice through a great part of North America, giving a particular account of the Origin, Government, Laws and Customs of the *Gipsies*, and a Dictionary of the Cant Language used by the Mendicants. *Plate.* 12*mo, boards, uncut.* London, 1827

691 COOPER, MYLES. National Humiliation and Repentance recommended, and the Causes of the Present *Rebellion in* AMERICA, assigned in a *Sermon* preached before the University of Oxford, on Friday, December 13, 1776, etc., by MYLES COOPER, LL.D., President of KING'S COLLEGE, NEW YORK, etc. 4*to, pp.* 24. Oxford, at the Clarendon Press, 1777

View of King's College, (Columbia College) inserted.

692 DAVIS, WILLIAM J., AND DAWSON, HENRY B. Reminiscences of the CITY OF NEW YORK AND ITS VICINITY. *Plates.* 12*mo, uncut.* New York, 1855

50 COPIES ONLY PRIVATELY PRINTED. *Very scarce.*
Presentation copy to WASHINGTON IRVING.

693 [GRANT, MRS.] Memoirs of an *American Lady;* with

Sketches of Manners and Scenery in *America*, as they existed previous to the *Revolution.* 2 *vols., cr.,* 8*vo, boards, uncut.* London, 1817

694 Hinton, John Howard. History and Topography of the United States. Illustrated with a Series of Views, drawn on the spot, and engraved on steel. 100 *Fine plates.* 2 *vols.,* 4*to, boards, uncut.*
Original Edition. London, 1830

The plates include beautiful views of the New York Battery, Columbia College, Fort Ticonderoga, Lake George, The Palisades, Chestnut St. Theatre, Phila., Walnut St. Theatre, Phila., Masonic Hall, Broadway, etc.

695 Jefferson. Original Autograph Letter of Thomas Jefferson, to Judge Page, of Virginia. 1 *page,* 4*to.* Philadelphia, October 31, 1775

Unsigned. Of great Historical interest, says, "Gen. Montgomery and our forces before St. John, etc., have repelled three different attacks from the Fort, etc., etc." *Accompanying this letter are* 5 *Portraits of Jefferson, some very rare, including a fine original drawing.*

696 Johnson. Original Autograph Letter of Sir William Johnson, 1 *page,* 4*to.* "*Johnson Hall,* 24*th January,* 1767, *with rare Portrait.*

Fine Specimen.

697 Lafayette. Complete History of the Marquis De Lafayette, Major General in the Army of the United States of America, in the War of the Revolution; with account of his Tour through the United States, in 1825. By an officer in the late Army. *Two Portraits, view of* "*landing of Lafayette at Castle Garden,*" *etc. Fine original autograph letter of Layfayette inserted.* 8*vo, calf.* New York, 1826

698 Lee. Girdlestone, Thomas. Facts tending to prove that General Lee, was never absent from this Country, for any length of time, during the years, 1767,

1768, 1769, 1770, 1771, 1772, and that *he was the Author of* JUNIUS. *Rare Portrait of Gen. Charles Lee, (full length, with his Dog,) taken from a caricature drawing, by Barham Rushbrooke, Esq., also Fac-similes.* 8vo, *pp*, 138, *boards uncut, rough edges. Fine clean copy. Very scarce.* . London, 1813

699 MISCELLANEA CURIOSA. A Collection of Curious *Travels, Voyages, Antiquities, and Natural Histories* of Countries, etc., as delivered to the Royal Society. *Plates, Fac-similes, etc.* 3 *vols.* 8*vo, calf.* London, 1726

The third volume contains Clayton's Account of Virginia, and other matter relative to America.

700 NATIONAL PORTRAIT GALLERY OF DISTINGUISHED AMERICANS. Conducted by James Herring, New York, and James B. Longacre, Philadelphia, under the Superintendence of the American Academy of Fine Arts. 144 *Portraits of Statesmen, Soldiers, Authors, etc., etc.* 4 *vols.* 4*to. morocco, gilt.*

LARGE PAPER. *Rare.* Philadelphia, 1834–35–36–39

Morrell, uncut, $13.00 per vol.

701 NORTHERN INVASION OF OCTOBER 1780. A Series of Papers relating to the Expeditions from Canada under Sir John Johnson and others against the FRONTIERS OF NEW YORK, which were supposed to have *Connection with Arnold's Treason.* Prepared from the Originals, with an Introduction and Notes, by Franklin B. Hough. *Map and Plate. Royal* 8*vo, uncut.*

75 COPIES PRIVATELY PRINTED. New York, 1866

Bradford Club Series, No. 6.

702 REBELLION. EVANS, MRS. Silas Marner, the Weaver of Raveloe. 12*mo, pp.* 276. Mobile, 1863

Covers made of *Wall-paper.*

703 SEWARD, ANNA. Beauties of, Carefully Selected and Al-

phabetically arranged under appropriate heads. By W. C. Oulton. *Fine Portrait of Miss Seward, engraved by Woolnoth, after Romney.* 12*mo, boards, uncut.* London, 1822

704 SMITH, JOSHUA HETT. An Authentic Narrative of the Causes which led to the Death of *Major André*, Adjutant-General of his Majesty's Forces in North America. To which is added a Monody on the Death of Major André, by Miss Seward. *Map and View of André's Monument in Westminster Abbey.* 8*vo, half calf.* London, 1808

Has fine Portrait of André inserted, but wants the one belonging to the book.

☞ LARGE BLACK WALNUT BOOKCASE, *glass doors, with drawers,* will be sold on WEDNESDAY EVENING, JANUARY 13th, AT 8 O'CLOCK.

www.ingramcontent.com/pod-product-compliance
Lightning Source LLC
LaVergne TN
LVHW011234110826
845150LV00006B/1633